THE BIGGER GAME
Why Playing a Bigger Game
Designs Who You Want to Become

Laura Whitworth
Rick Tamlyn
and Caroline MacNeill Hall

Outskirts Press, Inc.
Denver, Colorado

Outskirts Press, Inc.
http://www.outskirtspress.com

ISBN: 978-1-4327-2416-0

Library of Congress Control Number: 2009923782

Outskirts Press and the "OP" logo are trademarks belonging to Outskirts Press, Inc.

PRINTED IN THE UNITED STATES OF AMERICA

Acknowledgements

Since 2001, the Bigger Game has grown, changed, and morphed – just as Bigger Games are supposed to. There have been countless Bigger Game players along the way, each helping in their own way with the creation of this book.

We would like to thank Savoula Lidis, Alan Roe, LA Reding, Susan Valdiserri, Leslie Clark, and Bob Johnson for their early guidance and wisdom.

We thank Melissa O'Mara, Pat Obuchowski, Barbara Key, Bruce Tamlyn, Jenn Weinberg, Jim Bower, Dinesh Salve, Peggy Wallis, Margo Bebinger, Debby Doig, Nancy Allen, Amy Filipek, Sherry Hill, Norma Dompier, Ann Jameson, Kirsten McKinnon, Anna Freitas, and Lloyd Ziel – all early Bigger Game players.We also thank Karen Kimsey-House, Henry Kimsey-House, and The Coaches Training Institute.

Dori Ben-Chanock, Jeffrey Corbett, Sharna Fey, Deborah Huisken, Jon Benfer, Deborah Colman, Andy Denne, Jeff Jacobson, Mike Kulczyk, Conner Loomis, Martyn Lowesmith, Lauren Powers, Nancy Sarah, Knut Leo, Cathy Manning, Nina McGuffin, Rich Raffals, and Diane Wendt all became trained in the first Bigger Game training program – we thank them for standing by us and for teaching *us* a thing or two along the way.

Thank you to Judy Pike and Isha for their ongoing support and love. And to Chuck Lioi, who continues to be a wizard at keeping it all going.

And a special thank you to the thousands of Bigger Game players who have taken our workshops and trainings around the globe.

Dedication

This book is dedicated to the memory of Laura Whitworth. Laura's wisdom, fire, compassion, and zest for life are truly missed.

Contents

Introduction

"What makes a human being dare the impossible? What fires the will when we glimpse something never done before and a wild urge surges up to cry, 'Then let's do it'?

...Human beings cannot live without challenge. We cannot live without meaning. Everything ever achieved we owe to this inexplicable urge to reach beyond our grasp, do the impossible, know the unknown. This urge is part of our evolutionary heritage, given to us for the ultimate adventure: to discover for certain who we are, what the universe is, and what is the significance of the brief drama of life and death we play out against the backdrop of eternity...

You are what your deep, driving desire is.
As your desire is, so is your will.
As your will is, so is your deed.
As your deed is, so is your destiny."

– from the Introduction to The Upanishads, *as translated by*
Eknath Easwaran

i

This sacred writing is exactly what the Bigger Game is all about. The Bigger Game is based on the belief that we all hunger for a fulfilling life – a life filled with meaning and purpose – for ourselves and for the people around us.

The late Laura Whitworth and Rick Tamlyn co-created the Bigger Game. Caroline MacNeill Hall, a co-player, has been an ally in bringing this model to the world. They have witnessed, over and over again, "ordinary" people doing extraordinary things – and subsequently pursuing even greater challenges and contributions once they discovered what they're passionate about. These ordinary people are playing what we call a Bigger Game.

This book introduces the Bigger Game – a revolutionary change and innovation model – and shows you how you can find your own Bigger Game. We believe that if you fully embrace the model and its philosophy, you will accomplish extraordinary results in your life... and for our world.

The Bigger Game is seemingly simple, and is laid out to resemble a classic tic-tac-toe game. But don't be fooled by its simplicity. The logic of the Bigger Game unfolds with richness, complexity, and depth as you play it and grow from it.

The birth of the model: Laura Whitworth's Bigger Game
Laura Whitworth, who died of lung cancer in February 2007, became a Bigger Game player (although she hadn't called it that) back in 1988. Here's how it all got started in her own words:

"I had taken some personal growth workshops and believed passionately that 'coaching' conversations could help people sort out what was important in their lives. So I left the comfort zone of being an employee and I started a business that I called *Personal and Professional Coaching*. What a gulp that was!

One of my very first clients was Henry House, who became a coach and a friend. Together, we saw an opportunity to train other coaches and decided to create a workshop to do so. All of a sudden, I had to leave another comfort zone and learn how to lead workshops. Another gulp! After Henry and I delivered our first workshop, people requested more. I thought, 'Ommigod, how do we do this?' We were making things up as we went along.

We soon recruited another ally in Karen Kimsey (who would later marry Henry) and the three of us took a deep breath and started The Coaches Training Institute (CTI). Our wildest ambition was to someday offer one workshop a month. Before long, we had accomplished that goal and more. (At this writing, The Coaches Training Institute is the largest coaching training school in the world.)

Fast forward to June 2000. Karen and I were invited to teach coaching skills in a federal prison in Englewood, Colorado, as part of a program that trained inmates to counsel juvenile offenders. We found that many of the inmates simply did not know how to have a conversation that wasn't confrontational. As we worked with them, they learned new ways to think about others, to experience their own feelings, and to interact in a healthy, generous way. They were so hungry to learn. It was deeply inspiring.

I realized right then and there that the 'coaching approach' could give people around the world a way to relate to one another from respect and curiosity rather than from blame or judgment. I saw that we could play a pivotal role in saving the planet, and the prisons were the perfect place to start. Englewood had been a one-time workshop. We needed to do more. We had to get back into the prisons with our training. We just had to, and yet I didn't know how.

I knew I needed to make some investments first. I was exhausted and physically depleted. I had known for a long time that I 'should' quit smoking. Now there was no choice in the matter. So I quit. Cold turkey. I would be in a terrible state of agitation and anxiety, craving a cigarette, and I would think about Gary or Keith or Russ – all inmates I knew at the prison. This agony was worth it for them.

I spent the next few months recruiting allies to help me take coaching back inside the prison system. As we talked about how to raise money, we came up with an idea for a one-day workshop, proceeds from which would go to the prison work. In the first workshop, in December 2001, we laid out the first draft of what we called the Bigger Game model, a new way for humans to learn and grow. Five workshops later, we had raised $60,000 to support coaching training in prisons.

I noticed something hugely exciting as we moved the prison project forward. The key players in the project were growing by leaps and bounds, including me. Oh my, I was so intimidated by the work! And yet, the purpose was so compelling that it dragged me out of my comfort zones, kicking and screaming. Again and again, I got scared as I took bold steps into thin air without knowing if support would rise beneath my feet. It just had to happen…and it did! And I became a different person because of it.

The prison project mattered hugely, and I had fielded a team of committed co-players to carry the work forward. This gave me the opportunity to shift my focus and think about what I wanted to do next. I realized it was the Bigger Game model itself. The model was emerging as a reliable tool for connecting with 'Oh my God, this just has to happen!' I was on fire about the Bigger Game and its potential to change the world. And yet, I didn't know how.

That was the point when I reached out to Rick Tamlyn, one of CTI's most senior leaders, with the idea of bringing the Bigger Game into organizations. Together, we continued to morph and grow the model. Without knowing how in advance, we brought a combination of the Bigger Game and coaching training to one of the world's most-respected technology companies, which framed it as 'a new style of leadership.'"

Rick Tamlyn's Bigger Game
In Rick Tamlyn's last year of high school in New Jersey, he was elected to head his church youth group. Traditionally, the group's get-togethers had focused on bowling and pizzas, and everybody was fine with that. But Rick had a vision of doing something a little more meaningful. He was only 16 years old, but a yearning to get away from business as usual and move toward something with more heart and meaning fired him. Here's what Rick did in his own words:

"I remember sitting down with the minister of my church and saying that I wanted to do something that would have huge impact on others. We brainstormed together and came up with the idea of taking 35 members of my youth group down to Annville, Kentucky, over spring vacation to build homes for the people of the Appalachian Mountains.

We had no idea how we were going to do this when we made the commitment to do it. Through car washes and bake sales, we raised the money to buy plane tickets. We recruited carpenters to join the team and teach us home-building skills. The project involved recruiting allies on every front. So I learned how to inspire people to join us – the other kids, the youth group sponsors, potential donors.

When our group arrived in Annville, we encountered people whose life situations couldn't have been more different from ours. As we helped bring running water in their houses for the first time, the people would invite us to share the best meals they could provide. I was deeply moved by their graciousness and gratitude. And there was such compelling camaraderie and conversation among us high school kids. You can't imagine how much we learned about the world and about ourselves.

When we returned to New Jersey, the church elders asked me to speak about the experience. I was 17 years old when I stood up in front of the entire church and showed pictures and laughed and cried – and the congregation laughed and cried right along with me. The place was completely alive. It was the best speech of my life. The experience marked the beginning of my career as a keynote speaker and a coach who routinely wakes and shakes people up through enthusiasm, passion, and sense of humor. And, although I didn't know it at the time, it was the beginning of my career as a joyful Bigger Game player.

That experience designed me. When we started, I didn't know how to do it. I was just called by my hunger and the 'how' part fell into place afterwards. It was the first time I really got a taste of what I was capable of doing when I put my mind and heart behind it and boy, did I ever want more!"

Are you ready to play a Bigger Game?
Do you want more? Are you hungry for something to be different? Do you want to make a difference, and you're not sure how? Do

you challenge the status quo? Are you ready to risk? Do you see a different and better future? Are you hungry for meaning and purpose?

If you answered "yes" to any of the above questions, you are ready to play a Bigger Game.

This book is meant to inspire and grow you, and it will point you toward finding your own Bigger Game. More important, though, it will point you toward becoming a Bigger Game *player*, someone who is always looking simultaneously outside yourself and deep inside to create change – by expressing and growing your talents in service of what you care about most.

Playing a Bigger Game as a way of life is thrilling, sometimes scary, and very fulfilling. It is *big fun*. It uses everything you've got and asks for more. It is often far from comfortable; yet playing a Bigger Game pulls you forward into the most exhilarating experience you're ever likely to have.

Section One
What is a Bigger Game?

Paul Newman was a movie star with all the recognition, respect, and creature comforts the world has to offer. He hungered to find out how else he could contribute, and began making salad dressing, using the proceeds to support the environmental causes that were dear to his heart. Today there is an empire of high-quality food bearing the Newman's Own label, with enormous revenues going toward worthy causes. Paul Newman was a Bigger Game player.

Nelson Mandela began his life as a privileged farm boy and eventually became a freedom fighter, convict, and finally the leader of his nation who has done more than anyone on earth to end apartheid in South Africa. Nelson Mandela keeps playing Bigger Games.

Ted Turner is a classic repeat entrepreneur. His many ventures and adventures included the reinvention of buffalo ranching and bringing sailing's prestigious America's Cup back to the US in 1977 by designing and racing a revolutionary new yacht, the *Courageous*. In 1980, he focused his considerable appetite on challenging the three major television networks via an all-news cable television channel he called "CNN." Many people said it couldn't be done... it wouldn't work. Turner proved them wrong by tapping into the public's insatiable hunger for more and better news. Turner was *Time Magazine*'s Man of the Year in 1991 and now is president of the Turner Foundation, which addresses population and environmental issues. Ted Turner is a Bigger Game player.

Many Bigger Game players are people who aren't so famous; they are ordinary people whose hunger moves them to do extraordinary things. For example, ten years ago, Maureen Beauregard sought to end homelessness in Manchester, New Hampshire, by finding a way to shelter five women in a rented space. Her group, Families in Transition, now has a 330-unit permanent housing complex and thrift store. Maureen Beauregard is a Bigger Game player.

When Alcoholics Anonymous co-founders Dr. Bob and Bill W. first met, they were drunks whose doctors had told them that if they did not quit for good, they would soon die from liver damage. The two not only managed to get sober; they created the 12-Step Recovery program that has inspired and supported recovering addicts in more than 150 countries around the world. Dr. Bob and Bill W. played a Bigger Game.

Rosalie Campbell's regular visits to a Southern California women's prison hatched Garden Path Ministries, which helps to restore hope among inmates in seven prison facilities and three recovery centers in California, Arizona, and Texas. Rosalie Campbell is a Bigger Game player.

The movies are full of true stories about ordinary people who are called to extraordinary accomplishments by their circumstances. Heroines like whistle-blowers Karen Silkwood and Erin Brockovich and union leader Norma Rae. Bigger Game players all.

When artists Jonathan Sisson and Chris Hand moved into a depressed neighborhood in Minneapolis in 1990, they didn't feel safe no matter how many locks they had on the door. The stretch of Pleasant Avenue on which they lived was known as a "crack street," a haven for crime, filled with young people with nothing to do but get into trouble. Sisson and Hand wanted to feel safe in their neighborhood. So they recruited several youths from local street gangs and together built 90 Adirondack-style deck chairs, which they painted green. One night, the team loaded all the green chairs into a rental truck and delivered them in front of each home in a two-block area of the neighborhood. As residents emerged from their apartments, they gasped in wonder at their new furniture. By that evening, neighbors were lounging in their chairs, firing up charcoal grills, and having what amounted to a giant block party. The artists were never scared again – and the "Green Chair Project" evolved to become a nonprofit organization that teaches entrepreneurial skills to street youth and makes neighborhoods safer throughout the Twin Cities. Jonathan Sisson and Chris Hand are Bigger Game players.

Corporations play Bigger Games – games that go far beyond simply making a profit for shareholders. For example, Southwest Airlines is committed to democratizing the skies by becoming the low-cost alternative for air-travelers and the world's best company to work for. Google is not only reorganizing the way the world gains access to information (no small game, that), but is also committed to providing its computer scientists with challenges so complex and fascinating that they will keep them deeply engaged for a decade or more. Twenty years ago, supercomputer giant Cray Research set out to make the biggest, fastest scientific computers in the world – and succeeded. Wal-Mart has undertaken a massive organics and sustainability initiative for employees and customers alike. These companies are playing Bigger Games.

Whatever the impetus for playing a Bigger Game, becoming a Bigger Game player matters. Why? *Because Bigger Games are what change the world from what it is now to what it could be.* Yes, that's a lofty claim. And yet, it is proven true all the time, as people no different from you and me leave indelible handprints on their companies, their communities, their neighborhoods, their countries, and their planet.

And becoming a player also matters because it *changes you from who you are to who you potentially could be.* Playing a Bigger Game is about being absorbed in something worthy and hot that pulls on your soul and lights up your life.

What else is it? Where do the ideas come from? What does it

take to be a player? How do games change over time? What impact does playing have on the players? On the world? Lots of questions. The next four chapters offer some answers to what a Bigger Game is, what it takes to be a player, and why we all should care.

Chapter 1
Defining the Bigger Game

Becoming a Bigger Game player starts with knowing what a Bigger Game is, as well as what it isn't. In this chapter, we'll define the concept and start pointing you toward becoming a player.

Think of the word "game" as a metaphor for whatever you are doing in life. Some games are conscious choices, like applying to college, pursuing a specific profession, joining the Peace Corps, or becoming a parent. The games we have chosen in the past helped define who we are today. Other games have been forced upon us, such as being fired or promoted, having a devastating illness, getting divorced, winning the lottery, or needing to care for aging parents. These games shaped us, too – especially in the ways we rose to the occasion.

Now, you already know a lot about Bigger Game play. You've seen plenty of examples in the world. Putting the first man on the moon. Cleaning up a corporate waste site. Changing carbon emission standards to decrease global warming. Creating a corporate responsibility initiative. Campaigning to end world hunger. Working to get healthier food into school cafeterias. Launching socially responsible and/or green business ventures. Starting a local neighborhood watch. Ending apartheid. Bigger Games are everywhere. They come in all shapes and sizes. Each is different in content and, at the same time, very similar in form. Underlying all these games are nine common elements and a few key principles. We'll be explaining the nine common elements in the next chapter, but first, let's further define a Bigger Game.

Webster's Collegiate Dictionary has many definitions for "game," yet the ones below resonate with us the most:
Game (noun): activity engaged in for diversion or amusement; a procedure or strategy for gaining an end; a field of gainful activity; a field of play
Game (verb): to play for a stake
Game (adjective): having a resolute, unyielding spirit; willing to proceed

Beyond *Webster's*, we offer this umbrella definition: A Bigger Game is whatever you undertake in your life that has an impact on who you are becoming. Your games take place everywhere and can include your family, your community, your (or your children's) school, your network of relationships, your business, your industry, the national political scene, the environment, the arts, international relations, or wherever else you are involved and want to have an impact.

By virtue of your involvement – or non-involvement – in the games of your life, you grow as a human being, shrink, or don't change at all (which is pretty much the same as shrinking). That's why the foundation of the Bigger Game is this premise:

Playing a Bigger Game designs who you want to become.

The games we share
Consider for a moment some of the common games most of us have experienced in our lives. School is definitely one of them.

Were you an A student? A varsity athlete? On the debate team? In the band? Smoking cigarettes in the parking lot? Too cool for school? The school game may have been thrust upon you (as many games are), but you were able to choose how you wanted to play it. And who you became by the end of your educational career was an outcome of that choice.

Then there's the game of work. Have you taken jobs that "make sense" or do you routinely bite off whopping challenges that use everything you've got and then some? Are you strategic about leaving a position when you've learned all you can from what you're doing? Do you tend to stick with your established competencies and salary? There's no right or wrong here. Just notice that the game of work you've been playing has helped shape who you are today.

There are many other games that pretty much choose you – although you do have considerable say in the particulars (such as who will be your partner in the game of marriage). And then there are the games that you consciously choose because they matter so much to you.

Proud moments, big games
Consider some of the defining moments of your life – times when you decided to step up to a challenge and it changed you in some fundamental way. For example, Laura Whitworth chose to pioneer a profession called coaching and later took it into the American prison system. She was never again the security-oriented accountant she was back in the day. Rick Tamlyn was instrumental in transforming a youth group previously focused on bowling and pizza into a crack building team dedicated to improving lives. He transformed himself into a compelling public speaker in the process. Twenty years later, he introduced the Bigger Game to some of the biggest corporations in the world. Is he a different person because of this? Oh yes. Rick is a player.

We all have proud moments, defining moments that helped shape who we are today. How about the time you were poised at the end of a diving board, took a deep breath, executed a perfect half-gainer, and won the diving championship for your team? The time you organized your son's birthday party around a trash pick-up along a local highway? The time you worked tirelessly for your city councilwoman's reelection campaign and she won despite stiff competition? The times you scared yourself? The times you amazed yourself with what you could do? The times you found out what you were made of in the process of contributing to others?

Growing you, serving others

You may have surmised that what makes a game bigger is not so much its scope and magnitude but rather the extent to which it makes *you* bigger. A Bigger Game uses everything you've got and asks for more. In the process of delivering the more, you become more capable, more resilient, more resourceful, more of a leader... bigger!

And Bigger Games tend to serve others. Let's look at an example. Lance Armstrong was a super-competitive bicyclist. He won lots of races and pots of money and grew his skills day after day. He owned a big house and fast cars and was nice to his mother. He was a successful player, no question about it... but he wasn't playing a Bigger Game. He was winning for himself, and sometimes for his team. Nothing wrong with that, of course. Hurray for the game he was playing!

And then Lance Armstrong was diagnosed with testicular cancer. He fought the disease –complete with hellacious betrayals and remarkable support – to create a huge turnaround. And in the process, he discovered a fierce hunger in himself on behalf of the cancer sufferers of the world. He committed himself to helping others approach the battle from a perspective of hope and empowerment and to finding a cure.

In order to help cancer patients fight winning battles with the right attitude, Armstrong wrote a book. Along the way, he launched the Live Strong Foundation and funded it by selling millions of yellow rubber bracelets. And he kept getting huge visibility for his foundation by riding his bike faster than anybody else on the planet. But bike racing was no longer a "self game." It was and is part of a Bigger Game, which continues to grow. Bike racing became an investment in the Bigger Game player – Lance became a

symbol, spokesperson, and inspiration for cancer survivors everywhere. He has mobilized many allies, via the Lance Armstrong
Foundation, and continues to look for the right opportunities to
find a cure.

A Bigger Game is one that your higher self wins

Okay, here's where we are so far. A Bigger Game is an endeavor
that grows you while it benefits others. Let's qualify that even further, because there are a number of things that grow your skills and
benefit others that qualify as big games, but not as bigger ones. For
a game to qualify as "bigger," it has to be beyond your current capabilities. In other words, if you already know how to do it, it isn't
a Bigger Game.

For example, back when Lance Armstrong was simply a bike
racer, he knew what he was doing. When he started his foundation,
though, he didn't know anything about philanthropy. He had to
learn how to launch a foundation and fund it for the sake of his
game.

You'll notice that the starting point here is not what you're already good at (which is how a lot of us end up in the jobs we occupy). Rather, the starting point is what you care about madly. If
you care enough, you'll figure out how to acquire – or ally with –
the skills you need in order to move the game forward. It is important that your Bigger Game asks for your best self *and* that's not
the key determinant for choosing it. After all, Lance Armstrong
didn't start his Bigger Game by saying to himself, "Gee, I think I'd
be good at starting a foundation, selling gazillions of yellow rubber
bracelets to kids all over the world, and buoying up cancer patients
with hope and courage." He founded the foundation because it
mattered so much to him – because he simply had to.

A Bigger Game is a team sport

For a game to qualify as a Bigger Game, it has to involve other
people; if you can do it all by yourself, it's a *self game*. In a bike
race, Lance Armstrong may be the person we see speeding across
the finish line, but he is backed mile after mile by a skilled support
team. Similarly, the Live Strong Foundation could not have come

into being or continue to function without the cooperation, commitment, and support of co-players and allies – and lots of them.

The intersection of your hunger and the world's hunger
A Bigger Game must also represent the place where your personal hunger intersects with a hunger in some part of your world – your community, church, or organization. We call these realms or domains of your life *"the field."* Let's say you yearn to paint the streets green because you *really* like that color. Or to bring Beanie Babies to work so you and your colleagues can juggle them in the cafeteria at lunchtime and have some laughs. But unless everybody in the neighborhood yearns for green streets and all your colleagues hunger to lighten up at lunch, you're responding to a personal desire that doesn't mesh with the hunger in the field. The result is a self game every time. Self games aren't bad; they just aren't "bigger."

Conversely, there may be a hunger in the field that you certainly believe in – ending famine in Africa, for example – and yet it's not the hunger that fires your soul. So, send a check, write to your congresswoman, sign a petition... but this isn't *your* Bigger Game. Your Bigger Game emerges from a hunger in the field that intersects with what you want fiercely for yourself.

Outgrowing your game
Something else that's true about Bigger Games is that they tend to evolve quite rapidly. Let's say you started playing a Bigger Game last year when you were promoted to second line manager and took your department to record levels of customer satisfaction. It was scary because you didn't know how to do it when you started and you had to figure it out along the way. You needed every member of your team pulling together to get there. And your combined efforts benefited your customers in ways your company had never even approached before. It was truly a Bigger Game.

But now it isn't. Why? Because you did it already, you know how to do it, and you could do it again. Great! It's well worth duplicating. But it's not growing you anymore. That's the thing about Bigger Games. As your game grows you, you outgrow it, and it's time to find the next challenge. You want to! It's so much fun to discover what you can do and how you can contribute. That's what drives repeat Bigger Game players like Ted Turner and Nelson Mandela. They can't wait to get out of bed each morning for the thrill of the game. And if you are attending to your hunger, the hunger in the field, and the quality of your character, your Bigger Game will continue to change until the day you are laid to rest, at which point your tombstone can read: "Realized My Potential."

Being a player
"Didn't make waves." "Always drove late model cars." "Got enough sleep." "Usually had something tasty for dinner." "He was nice." Those are possible epithets, too, you know. But nobody really wants to be remembered for those qualities. The fact is... human beings want to have meaningful lives. Once the basics of survival are handled, we want to contribute, to create, to have lives that matter to other people. Being a Bigger Game Player – using the model to orient us around working our current game and/or finding the next one – is an especially effective and simple way to do that. You see, it doesn't matter whether or not you have a Bigger Game at the moment. What's important is simply that you are a *player*, looking for the next opportunity that lights you up and develops your character and capabilities.

The Bigger Game and the highest good
It is no exaggeration to say that Bigger Games are responsible for the evolution of human civilization and all the advances in human history. Think about it. A Bigger Game is called into being by the union of "what I want" and "what is wanted" in the field. A Bigger Game is an act of creation: It is so challenging that you have to master new skills and qualities in order to accomplish it. A Bigger Game is an act of contribution: It advances human lives in one way or another. A Bigger Game requires collaboration and cooperation, which are the basis of human socialization. And a challenge of this caliber promotes a level of aliveness and engagement that brings out the best in us.

Gallup studies show that engagement is a key factor in successful leadership and in business results. There are a number of best-selling business books on this subject these days, including *The Power of Full Engagement* by Jim Loehr and Tony Schwartz and Stephen Covey's *The Eighth Habit*, which focuses on finding one's voice. Those employees who are highly engaged are the ones who drive corporate change. And the Bigger Game is a powerful approach that works toward aligning and engaging employees in the change that matters most to them. In fact, we can point to the Bigger Game as a potent force for corporate innovation. It represents the "pull forward," as opposed to traditional change management approaches that tend to view change as something to be resisted.

There is even a hint of spiritual transcendence here since playing a Bigger Game leads us into "flow," a wholly focused and engaged state of being that "provides a sense of discovery, a creative feeling of transporting the person into a new reality," says Mihaly Csikszentmihalyi, author of *Flow: The Psychology of Optimal Experience*. Being in flow, he asserts, "pushes the person to higher levels of performance and leads to previously undreamed-of states of consciousness." In other words, it's your highest self that is the Bigger Game player.

Given that the stakes are essentially the continuing evolution of humankind, then, it is critical that the team of Bigger Game players in our world continues to create new members. The good news is that the moment we *commit* to being a Bigger Game player is the moment we start playing a Bigger Game, whether we have identified the game or not. That's right. If the desire is there, we're already playing!

Summary

A "game" is broadly defined as what we are up to in various parts of our lives. "Playing a Bigger Game designs who you want to become" is the foundation of the model. The games we play in our lives shrink us, grow us, or mire us in the status quo.

A Bigger Game:
• is precisely the opposite of "business as usual."

• is an endeavor in which the challenge is much greater and the stakes much higher than the games you've played before.

• is the product of the union between your fierce personal hunger and the hunger of "*the field*" – your community, organization, world, etc.

• is something you choose deliberately because it so compels you.

• is a challenge that's beyond your current capabilities, thus demanding that you blast out of comfort zones and stretch to meet it.

• calls for bold action.

• serves you and something greater than yourself.

• requires a team to make it happen – it's so much bigger than just one person.

• changes over time as you outgrow what once seemed daunting and look toward the next place to stretch.

• is for the highest good of all.

• is totally worth it.

• is wildly fun!

Chapter 2
Working the Bigger Game Board

We have asserted that the Bigger Game doesn't have anything to do with winning. Rather, it is more about a way of life in which you consistently show up as a player. The moment you choose to pursue a life of meaning and success – and say "no" to business as usual – you've started to play a Bigger Game. The only prerequisite for being a player is your desire for something more. It's fine if you don't have a specific Bigger Game yet. That game – and the games after that – will ensue in due course if you are awake to the process and allow yourself to dream big and yearn hard.

The bottom line is that the only requirements for starting to play a Bigger Game are hunger and desire. Welcome!

In this chapter, we'll be walking through the Bigger Game Board. The Bigger Game Board is composed of the nine elements of the model, and is laid out like a classic game of tic-tac-toe. We'll explore each element square by square, as if it were tidy and linear. It isn't. Most of us occupy several squares at once. In fact, the Bigger Game is more like the old parlor game Twister – or maybe Chutes and Ladders – than like a step-by-step, sequential game such as Monopoly. (The payoff can be even richer than owning multiple hotels, however.)

The top of the Game Board: the Name of your Game
You'll notice at the top of the Game Board the words "Play a Bigger

Game." This is just a placeholder title for the name of *your* Bigger Game. If you already know what that is, that's well and good. If you don't have a clue, that's fine, too. We'll be exploring *how* to find your own Bigger Game later in this book.

Comfort Zones

Comfort zones are our default behavior – our routines, habits, and patterns. Comfort zones are not necessarily comfortable; rather, they are familiar. Comfort zones are what we know. They are the ways we organize much of our lives.

A comfort zone is anything we do automatically, without having to think about it. All of us have comfort zones of action and comfort zones of thought. Examples of the former might include tooth-brushing, checking e-mail 20 times a day, daily television watching, exercising four times a week, a bowl of ice cream after dinner, reading bedtime stories to the kids, drinking coffee on the morning commute, smoking cigarettes on breaks, etc. Examples of the comfort zones of *thinking* include habitual thoughts of "I can" or "I can't," "Why stick my neck out?" or "Why volunteer, nothing will ever change" or "When will it ever stop changing?" and so on.

There's no getting away from comfort zones. The human propensity for establishing routines is hardwired into our genetic makeup. This is neither good nor bad. The fact is that many of our comfort zones serve us. At the same time, many do not. All comfort zones come with costs and payoffs. And there are some comfort zones so limiting that they cost us our Bigger Game. That's why it's almost always necessary to leave comfort zones if we are to be players.

Before you can choose to leave something, though, you have to know it exists. What makes comfort zones particularly insidious is that they are largely invisible. We're so accustomed to them that we see them as "just the way things are" or *the truth*. Playing on the Bigger Game Board requires that we actively notice when we are in a comfort zone –however seemingly benign it may be – and identify its costs and benefits so that we can choose whether to retain it or kick it to the curb. That means, of course, that there are times when we will find ourselves actually choosing discomfort for the sake of our Bigger Game and who we aspire to become. Bottom line: the Bigger Game asks you to examine your comfort zones and decide whether they serve your game or not.

Hunger

Spending too much time on automatic pilot creates entropy, stagnation, even depression. Remember that old Peggy Lee song "Is That All There Is?" Her advice to "stuck" people was just to "break out the booze, and have a ball." Well sure, that's one approach. Essentially, Lee would have us leapfrog from one comfort zone to another as a form of anesthesia. Another approach – and a pattern we like better, frankly – is that when people get tired of the same old routine (and themselves), they begin to hunger for something with more meaning, more purpose, a better reason to swing their legs over the side of the bed each morning. Hunger, uncomfortable as it may be, is a precious commodity. In fact, hunger is the most critical component of the Bigger Game Board. It is the fertile soil where Bigger Games take root.

Why? In a culture that instantly provides all the material amenities we could possibly want, we often lose touch with the deep desire of our souls. We may only want what we know we can get. Rather than risk failure, we tend to want what is safe. Hunger for what we don't have is an uncomfortable experience. When you want something badly and you don't have a clue how you're going to get it, the discomfort can be intense. In the cultures of developed nations, there are plenty of quick and easy ways to anesthetize us against the pain of unfulfilled hunger – fast food fixes or empty calories, if you will. The key to a fulfilling life, though, is to slow down and seek the hunger of the soul, allow it to grow, and allow it to growl. As a Bigger Game player, your job is to turn up the volume on hunger – to let yourself want what you want. For your colleagues, your company, your neighborhood, the world. Want what you want. Want it big and want it bad.

Where does the wanting come from? Sometimes a generic hunger for meaning grows when we tire of a life in which we think, "Is this all there is?" At these times, we go in search of something, not knowing what it is, yet clear that something is missing.

At other times, the wanting is more specific, stirring in response to a circumstance. A loss or tragedy can arouse hunger in a heartbeat. For example, when Patty Wetterling's son Jacob was abducted from their suburban neighborhood in St. Joseph, Minnesota, it awakened in her an overwhelming desire to protect all children from harm. Her nonprofit organization, the Jacob Wetterling Foundation, is the main reason that missing children began appearing on the side of milk cartons.

Then there are those golden opportunities – glimpses of possibility – that arouse a hunger we didn't know we had. For many a student, hunger is awakened in college. Astronomy 101 wakes up the yearning to colonize the galaxies out there and Psychology 101 to probe the depths of the human mind. History 202 firms our resolve to redress the mistakes of the past in our political system. We don't know what we don't know, until we do. And when we do, the fire of hunger is ignited.

As a Bigger Game player, there are two kinds of hunger you are listening for: the hunger within you, and the hunger out there in your world. A compelling purpose is the result of the union between these two hungers. And a compelling purpose is what provides a good enough reason to keep hungering, keep looking and listening, keep moving – even at those times when you're most tempted to retreat to the empty calories of familiar pleasures.

Compelling Purpose
Eradicate AIDS in the world so that no one I love will ever be affected by it again.

Transform the education system in Japan into a collaborative learning model where individual creativity is respected and encouraged (and my child can grow).

Identify and eliminate verbal abuse so that no woman is diminished by words (as I once was).

Transform the American political system to ensure equality for all, regardless of gender (so my daughter will be paid as much as my son for the same job).

These are examples of the union between your personal hunger and the hunger in the field. On the Bigger Game Board, the place where your hunger and the field's hunger intersect is where compelling purpose is born. This union has a powerful vibration that we call resonance. It is compelling, rich, meaningful, and has an impact that goes well beyond you. Compelling purpose is a response to your hunger and yet it is no longer about you. This purpose lives out there in the field and requires you to commit to something bigger than yourself. For your compelling purpose to generate your Bigger Game, it must be big enough to make you step outside your comfort zones and stretch yourself toward your very best. When you get overwhelmed and want to stop playing your Bigger Game, your purpose must be compelling enough so that you recover and stay the course.

Compelling purpose is about being "up to something big" that contributes to the highest good for all. Lest you think we are asking you to become a do-good altruist dedicated to self-sacrifice and pain, you should know that this is where the big fun begins. Why? Because when you take your attention off yourself and put it on what matters most to you and the desire to bring it to others, you get to experience your most powerful self. When you get out of your own way, it is as if you open a channel into your soul, and all the resources and intelligence you need are there for the taking.

The Buddhist concepts of suffering and joy are useful here. A major source of suffering, according to Buddhist teachings, is the experience of being alone – alone in your own mind, alone with your thoughts, disconnected from the world. Joy, on the other hand, is simply a matter of remembering that all human beings – and the entire world, for that matter - are connected. And what it takes to bring that memory to life is getting present and casting your attention "out there" as well as on yourself. Following this logic, acting on your compelling purpose is the greatest joy available to a human being.

Your compelling purpose represents what must happen, and serves a hugely important role on the Bigger Game Board. It is the reason and the fuel for playing the game. It's the "good enough reason" to step out of your comfort zones for the sake of the game. After all, you don't learn by doing what you already know how to do. We grow only by doing what we've never done before. We naturally balk at this, of course, because being competent is pleasant (comfortable!), so we need to have sufficient motivation to pull us toward the unknown, where we are less skilled and more awkward. Our compelling purpose evokes what is best and highest in us as we venture into unknown territory.

Gulp

Now, a compelling purpose such as "creating sufficiency and self-authority for all" is a thing of grandeur. It should be grand; it's your reason for being! And yet, grandeur is intimidating. "Who do I think I am?" one might think. "I don't know how. This is too big." Meet the gulp. The gulp is an unavoidable element of the Bigger Game, because when your purpose is big enough, it's going to be scary, no way around it.

The gulp arises because you know you must do something, but you don't know how. And yet you feel you must. You also know that your existing competencies aren't enough to ensure your success. The gulp happens when you begin walking into ambiguity, stepping into the void with no guarantee that a stepping-stone will appear beneath your feet. The gulp usually involves actual physical sensations, such as sweaty palms, knots in the stomach, a mouth so dry that it's hard to swallow. These sensations may be uncomfortable but they're also wonderful, because they mean you're on the right track. Some Bigger Game players actually describe the gulp more as a feeling of exhilaration. However it shows up for you, whether it's a rapid heart beat, fear, and/or exhilaration, it's a feeling that you will experience again and again as you play your game.

The gulp has two potential effects:
1) "This is too big. I can't!" It can paralyze you and send you scuttling back to what you already know, i.e., a comfort zone that doesn't serve you or your game.
2) The gulp can deliver the sweaty-palmed exhilaration of a roller

coaster ride: "Man oh man, we're climbing. This is big. I'm scared. This is cool. Here we gooooooo. Whoo hoo!"

Think about standing in the surf. There's a massive wave headed your way. You have a choice. You can stand there, paralyzed with fear, and the wave will knock you down and tumble you toward the beach, your pants full of sand. Or you can take a deep breath and dive into the wave, only to emerge, jazzed, on the other side. Let that choice be guided by your game!

Bigger Game players consciously choose to step out of their comfort zones, take a deep breath, and dive into the wave. It all starts with the gulp, fueled by purpose: "I don't know how, *yet this must be...* here I go!"

Investment

Once you know your compelling purpose, it's time to start investing, especially in you, the Bigger Game player. Look around your life. What do you need to clean up, to start or stop doing, and/or to learn in order to play a Bigger Game? Maybe you need to improve your health – give up cigarettes, hit the gym, bid sayonara to McDonald's. Maybe you need to get your office and your life organized so that you have a great place to work and time to do it in. Maybe you need to take classes or workshops to bolster your skills, or connect with experts in related fields. Maybe it's time to gather resources and start designing your strategy. Maybe it's time to hire an assistant, an accountant, a housekeeper, a personal trainer, and/or a chef. Maybe it's time to tend to your personal relationships to make your home life richer and more harmonious... to join Toastmasters... to book a wonderful adventure vacation that bolsters your joyous perspective on the world...

Your Bigger Game needs you to have energy, skills, and time to bring to the challenges before you. And commitment too. One important investment is simply to speak the name of your Bigger Game out loud at least five times a day. Your Bigger Game becomes more real every time you mention it. And it's important for you to hear yourself repeat it out loud, until your commitment is so strong and visible that there's no turning back.

Up until now, you've probably been telling yourself, "I should..." "I should take better care of myself," "I should clean up my office," "I should hire an assistant." Those "I shoulds" have a funny way of not happening when they're only about you. Once you're a Bigger Game player, though, it's not just about you anymore. Just as a pregnant woman needs to take good care of herself for the sake of the baby she is incubating, the game you're incubating needs you to invest in yourself. And you want that, too, because the game is your baby!

Allies

To play a Bigger Game, you'll need and want allies. If your game is big enough, it would be hard to go it alone. Furthermore, if you play all by yourself, how can your game go on without you when you're ready to move on to what's next?

Allies come in all forms. There are the allies you hire – lawyers, coaches, accountants, assistants, and other expert resources. There are your friends, listeners, and cheerleaders who think you're simply the greatest and invite you to talk about your Bigger Game so that you can hear yourself think. Then there are your co-players and co-leaders, others who are so committed that your Bigger Game becomes their own Bigger Game. Even your greatest critics can serve as allies when their nay-saying serves to strengthen your commitment and resolve. ("Hell no, you're not going to tell me I can't!") One hugely important ally is the person who agrees to "come in and get you" when your comfort zones are exerting an especially strong pull on you.

The most important allies of all, of course, are those your Bigger Game serves – your prospects, clients, audience, participants, beneficiaries. Metaphorically, they are calling out and reminding you of the hunger "out there" that met with your own hunger to manifest your compelling purpose in the first place.

The more allies you have, the more support and resources are available for your Bigger Game. The time to start recruiting, then, is now, even if you have not identified a specific Bigger Game yet. Remember, your allies can help you wake up your hunger and move toward your compelling purpose, too.

Sustainability

Your Bigger Game is a big deal. You want to make sure it can last over time. And you want to make sure you last, too. So the sustainability square of the Game Board focuses both on the sustainability and continued well-being of the Bigger Game player, as well as on the game itself. Yes, you are focusing on keeping yourself in the game, but if you were no longer there, are systems and resources in place so the game could go on without you? Once again, the game is too important for its survival to depend completely on you.

In the context of the Bigger Game, sustainability refers to the process known as systems thinking – considering the impact of cause and effect on the whole. The personal side of systems thinking points to the need for life balance. You don't want to be sacrificing your health, relationships, or financial well-being in order to play your Bigger Game. You need to attend to all areas of your life so you don't hyper-focus on the game and burn yourself out. The self-sacrifice that leads to burnout, by the way, simply undermines the game you care about and is ultimately about you. That's a comfort zone that can cost you your game.

Assess

The Bigger Game player must learn to assess where they are in relationship to the game. When you are able to assess, the opportunities for flexibility, creativity, and adeptness are increased.

"How am I doing?" I assess when I wake up in the morning to see where I am on the Game Board today. I assess what investments I need to make. I assess whether my compelling purpose still has the power to make me weak in the knees. I assess my effectiveness in recruiting the allies I need.

How is my Bigger Game doing? Is my strategy clear? Is it making progress? Is it still on target? On purpose? Is it still important? Aligned with my core values? Your Bigger Game will want to change and evolve pretty much constantly, so it's essential that you develop the ability to discern when comfort zones are driving you or when the game is driving you.

Of course, you can't measure how you're doing if you haven't defined what success will look like. Every Bigger Game must have a definition of success and a way to measure whether you've achieved it or not. That's why in the assess square of the Game Board, the focus is on the key results you're shooting for, your game plan for getting there, and milestone goals along the way.

Bold Action

The Bigger Game is not a change and innovation model that exists in a vacuum. It's about rising to a specific, urgent need and making things happen. Just thinking about it is not enough. Without bold action at the center of your Bigger Game, you have little more than a wish, a yearning, a good idea. Bold Action sits squarely in the center of the Game Board because it is required in virtually every square. Like the game of Twister, one foot is in the center, no matter where else your other foot – or your hands – might be. It takes bold action to leave a comfort zone, to allow yourself to get quiet enough to hear the murmuring of your soul. It takes bold action to envisage a compelling purpose and move forward in spite of the gulp. It takes bold action to recruit allies, invest in your development and preparedness, and assess where you are. And it takes bold action to make you and your game sustainable.

One of the great advantages of bold action is that it tends to vanquish the paralysis that often accompanies fear. Think of it this way: A Bigger Game is a gulp-worthy challenge, by definition. It probably scares you, at least a little. It is impossible, however, for fear and bold action to coexist in the same moment. Bold actions, by definition, require courage. Bestselling author M. Scott Peck in *The Road Less Traveled* writes this about fear and courage: "Courage is not the absence of fear, but the stepping out in spite of fear. Without fear, there is no courage."

Here's a metaphor for this concept. You're rafting down the Colorado River at the bottom of the Grand Canyon. You're in a peaceful stretch of water, but off in the distance, you begin to hear a roaring, whooshing sound that gets louder with each passing second. You feel little pangs of fear, fear of the rapids that surely lie ahead and what might happen to you when you get there. And yet you are compelled to ride this river, and you choose to move forward in service of that goal. This choice is an act of courage, and it is a bold action. As the roaring intensifies, the water gets smoother and faster, faster, faster... narrowing finally to a tongue of clear rapid flow. Your fear peaking, you are momentarily immobilized. And then, your raft drops 20 feet into the boil of rough water and your body responds, steering around rocks, aiming for the holes, avoiding the towering waves. You are fully present, fully engaged with navigating the challenges of each moment. There is no room for fear in your action here – only responsiveness and flow.

Action blasts you out of the immobility that often accompanies fear and anxiety. When in doubt, acting boldly will usually carry you to the next stretch of calm water. And the more you put this theory to the test by acting when you feel more like freezing, the easier it becomes to get yourself moving the next time.

Bold actions require energy and are essential to successful Bigger Game playing. In a Bigger Game, it often takes a "good enough reason" to pull us through the gulp into bold action. Your compelling purpose is the good enough reason, and it provides the fuel, courage, and energy for taking bold action. (Because otherwise, why bother?)

So there you have it, the Bigger Game Board.

Finding yourself on the Game Board

Take a moment now and look at the Bigger Game Board. Where are you? Are you aware of your habits and routines and what they sometimes cost you? Attuned to your hunger for yourself and your world? Seeing where you need to invest in your personal development? Notice where you are. Notice where you want to be.

Notice also your personal response to this model. Does it affirm the work you've been doing in the world already? Does it make you question whether you're burning all your time and energy on what really matters to you? Does it seem so obvious that you can't believe you didn't think of it yourself?

Wherever you are is the perfect place for you to be. Whatever your current perspective, whether you see yourself as a master Bigger Game player already, or whether you are still exploring the idea of a Bigger Game with trepidation, this book holds something for you. For those who feel in familiar territory, this book will challenge you to dig deeper, to assess your competencies and the quality and size of the games you're choosing. If you're one who finds the idea of Bigger Game playing a bit daunting, allow yourself to "play" on the Game Board, with the commitment only to try it on for size. For all readers, you will find a new lens through which to view your world, your work, and your choices.

Summary

• All it requires to be a Bigger Game player is an earnest desire to have a more meaningful and successful life and to become conscious about where you are – and where you need to be – on the Bigger Game Board.

• The Bigger Game Board is more like Twister than Monopoly. Players are usually occupying several squares at once.

• At the center of the Game Board is Bold Action, which partners with every other element to move your game forward.

• The squares of the Game Board include:

  - Comfort Zones - abandoning those routines that don't serve you or your game
  - Hunger - turning up the dial on wanting
  - Compelling Purpose - the place where the hunger in the field and your personal hunger come together
  - Gulp - Who, me? It's gotta be
  - Investments - in you, the player
  - Allies - if you don't need them, your game could probably be bigger
  - Sustainability - of you the player and of the game itself
  - Assess - How are you doing? How is the game going?

Chapter 3
Becoming a Bigger Game Leader

The way we see it, a Bigger Game is by the people – you need to attract, inspire, and retain allies, collaborators, and expert resources in order to move your Bigger Game from the idea stage to reality. And a Bigger Game is for the people – you can't serve, influence, or empower anyone who doesn't trust you or listen to you. A Bigger Game asks that we ally with other human beings, and very often it is specifically about serving, creating for, or growing other human beings.

That means you'll need to become an effective leader to play a Bigger Game – and you'll want to invest in developing your leadership skills to prepare for your game.

What is a leader? By our definition, a leader is someone who knows he or she has an impact and is responsible for it. Furthermore, a leader is one who decides to make a difference. His or her Bigger Game is this difference.

This chapter explores four core competencies that will help you succeed as a Bigger Game leader, which in turn will help you succeed in making your Bigger Game realized.

Core Competency #1: A Leader's Attention
We human beings are set apart from all other mammals by our ability to think and to know that we are thinking. In addition to our advanced mental processes, we also enjoy a form of consciousness in common with our mammalian relatives: We can feel what's going on in any given situation even when nobody is saying a word.

We use our thinking and our senses to pay attention to something or other – virtually all the time. In general, we direct our attention to one of three places:

1) Self focus
First, we focus our attention on our own thinking and physical experiences. Hmm, I'm hungry. Is there any sliced turkey left for a sandwich? Do I have time to run to the market before my 3:00 meeting? What will I wear to the meeting? Oh, I just thought of an additional agenda item and a point I want to make. I need to e-mail my colleague to make sure we're aligned on outcomes. He's been a little distant lately. Is it something I've done? I wish I were better at making my needs known without antagonizing him. With all the practice I've had, I ought to know how to do this by now.... Geez, what's wrong with me? Or maybe it's all his fault. Okay, I need to finish this memo. Concentrate.

Our ability to focus on our own thoughts is essential. Without it, we'd starve to death. We'd miss every meeting. Our socks would never match. And we'd never notice our own brilliant ideas. The consequence of putting our attention on the self, however, is that when we're focused narrowly on our own thinking, we're not paying attention to anything around us and we have only a limited sense of what's going on.

2) Focus on other
The second place human beings regularly put their attention is on other human beings, one person at a time. Mothers are attuned to hear their babies' cries. Lovers have eyes for only each other. Stu-

dents are riveted to the charismatic teacher. When we are focused on another person, we get a sense of what's going on with him or her, but we may not have a clue about what's happening everywhere else. Attention on only one other person is a relatively narrow focus.

3) Focus on the field
The third place we put our attention is on the field. The field includes physical locations and consists of the mood, attitude, emotions, and energy that exist all around us. Focusing on the field requires that we be fully present with a soft, expansive focus broad enough to take in both our visible surroundings and all the invisible yet tangible qualities of emotion and energy that exist in our area of attention.

Whether you're seeking a Bigger Game or you are already playing one, your attention needs to be on the field much of the time. Why? Because the field is where Bigger Games ignite, where a compelling purpose resonates, and where allies are enrolled. Assessing the field is a core requirement of a Bigger Game player.

Now, some people might protest that their attention is already on the field most of the time, that they couldn't escape reading the field even if they tried! It is true that we tend to be barraged – sometimes against our will – by sensory, mental, and emotional information. It is also true, though, that we tend to react to what we're experiencing in the field with opinions and judgments that snap our attention out of the present and back onto our own thoughts and ourselves.

In order to put and keep our attention on the field, we need to be students of presence, non-attachment (to our own opinions), and recovery (the ability to bring our attention right back to the field when it strays). We will be fleshing out these concepts further as this chapter continues to unfold.

Core Competency #2: Meet-Point-Dance
Rick Tamlyn created a simple yet powerful leadership model called Meet-Point-Dance, which teaches a person how to be more intentional in striving for a certain impact and increases the

chances of a desired outcome that a leader yearns to create.

If we want to have an impact on something we care about – and that's the whole point of playing a Bigger Game, after all – we need to start by "meeting" people where they are, or meeting the field where it is. "To meet" is to relate, to lean into, to actively connect, to wonder, to be curious and available and open – to be "over there," really listening to other people so we can experience their world from their vantage point. When people feel seen and heard, they begin to trust us and are willing to try following our lead. This concept of "meeting" requires putting your attention on the field and keeping it there.

At the heart of meeting is a powerhouse principle that is the foundation of effective leadership – that is, the importance of seeing and relating to people as people. That may seem simplistic to you, but think about it. All too often, when we have an agenda, we see other human beings as barriers to what we want to accomplish, as vehicles for advancing our agenda, or as having no importance – essentially as objects in relation to us and what we want. When our attention is focused on our own desires, and ourselves, it's easy to forget that other people have needs, hopes, dreams, fears, wants, sensitivities... just like we do. Meeting others involves seeing them as people, peers, and playmates. Treating people as human beings is a hugely respectful way of relating to others – and it builds trust like nobody's business. (The concept of "seeing people as people" is laid out in considerable detail in *Leadership and Self-Deception*, a powerful book by The Arbinger Institute.)

When you're playing a Bigger Game, you're aiming to change things, shake 'em up, move people somehow, somewhere. To do that, you will need to "point" them. "Let's try it this way." "Go there." "Will you please...?" "Here's what you need to do." "How about...?" Pointing is an integral part of the change process. The trouble is, when pointing is the first thing we do, it often backfires on us. For one thing, nobody likes unsolicited advice. More important, nobody is likely to do what you suggest unless they trust you. And what is it that makes people trust you? Their sense of being seen, heard, understood, and respected.

Now let's talk about joining the "dance." If you meet people well, they're likely to go where you're pointing... except when they don't. When people follow your lead, you can't predict what will happen next. Maybe they're on board. Maybe mutiny is stirring. Maybe the field is changing so rapidly that where you're pointing has become irrelevant. Your responsibility, then, is to stay present and keep meeting people where they are and reading the field so that you can make an effective next move. We call this dancing. "To dance" is to read the field, point the next move, stick around and sense the impact of your pointing, stay aware and alert and agile, and dance with whatever shows up in the moment. Your next move may be another meeting moment or another pointing moment. Reading the field lets you know what to do next.

Let's visit the game of tennis for an analogy. Say a player hits a sensational shot. While she is admiring her own fabulousness, her opponent whacks the ball back over the net, where it smacks our one-shot wonder on the forehead. Oops. Analysis: She pointed, and then forgot to keep her attention on the field and, as a result, failed to dance.

Let's try again. Our player hits another great shot. Great pointing. This time, she returns to center on the baseline, weight forward, bouncy, and ready to lunge in any direction to field her opponent's return. Her attention is out there on the other person, as well as on the strength of the breeze, the position of the sun, and all the other elements that will determine what happens next. When the ball rockets back, she dances forward to meet it with her best shot. Voila. She's no longer a one-shot wonder. She's a player!

In the first example above, the tennis player's focus shifted from field to self because she was congratulating herself on a good shot. She could just as easily have been castigating herself for a bad one. In either instance, the player's thoughts about her own impact trigger a shift of attention away from the field.

This shift happens all the time in the games of life, and Bigger Game playing is no exception. It's paradoxical: The key to effective dancing is to become more conscious of your impact so you can respond appropriately to what's happening in the field. So your job, then, is to get really conscious!

When you connect to people as people, meet them where they

are before pointing them where you want them to go, and then dance with the outcome, you will be the kind of player who wins at Bigger Games.

Core Competency #3: Assess versus Vote

As we've said, Bigger Game leadership requires focusing on the field. Only when you have a clear picture of *what is* can you make effective choices regarding *what's next*. That's why one of the contexts of the Bigger Game Board is "Assess." You will need to assess the field: How's the game going? What's needed now? Where are we in the plan?

In addition to assessing the field, you also need to assess yourself. Yes, that's right – you need to assess yourself! How excited are you with your Bigger Game? Are you still having fun? Are you taking care of yourself? What's the impact you're having? How are your relationships with family and friends? When you assess your game, all of this must be in the mix. If you're not looking out for Number One, your Bigger Game won't stand a chance.

As a Bigger Game player, you need to be assessing where you are all the time, and do it without voting. We define "voting" as layering your judgment and emotional reaction over your assessment of "what is." Assessing is neutral and dispassionate; it's just the facts (even if the fact is that in this moment, your Bigger Game seems to be going straight down the tubes). When you are assessing, you are fully present. Your vision is clear and focused on the field. You are not attached to your judgments and opinions. You can see the data without an emotional charge.

When you are "voting," however, your vision is clouded and you are attached to your thoughts about *you*. You are more focused on yourself than on what's happening in the field. Voting is often polarized thinking. This is good. That is bad. I hate that. I love that. I hate me. I love me. When you are voting, you are no longer resilient, resourceful, or present.

Think of it this way. Assessing equals discerning, while voting equals judging. Assessment opens up possibilities, while voting slams that door shut.

Here's another analogy from sports to demonstrate the difference between assessing and voting. At just ten inches wide, a racing rowing shell is considerably narrower than most people's rear ends. That means it is both hugely responsive and darned tipsy. The rower's ability to stay balanced hinges in part on assessing what's happening with the oars so she can calibrate the oar work. And since she's speeding through the water backward, she needs to assess her position constantly to avoid ramming a bridge abutment or a riverbank. The boat is so light that wind and waves have a major impact on balance, too. The rower must constantly assess each of these factors, adjust appropriately, and return to the field. My oar is dipping too deep. Calibrate. I'm too close to the bridge. Adjust course. My angle is unstable against these waves. Respond. The moment the rower breaks the assess/respond cycle with a vote – "My oar is dipping too deep..." "Man, after all this practice, how could I still be getting this wrong...?" – she gets hooked by her thinking, her balance is thrown off, and she finds herself taking a swim and the race lost. Rowers call this concept "keeping your head in the boat."

"Keeping your head in the boat" is all about returning to assessment. Assess, adjust, assess, adjust... your attention stays in the field. There's no way to do this perfectly, of course, but Bigger Game players learn to keep their heads in the boat more often than not. How? By accepting "assess" as a rule of engagement, catching themselves voting, and remembering to return to assess until it becomes a way of life. Simple as that (though not always easy).

Core Competency #4: A Leader's Intention

Where we focus our *attention* has a direct bearing on our people skills and on our resourcefulness. Similarly, where we focus our *intention* has a huge bearing on the outcomes we achieve and the "luck" we attract in the process. This concept has been around for thousands of years, and it's key to playing a successful Bigger Game.

Intention starts with gaining clarity about our desired outcome – what it is we want to create. A clear goal is the North Star that pulls us forward and keeps us on course. In the Bigger Game, our North Star is our compelling purpose. Once we're clear on the compelling purpose, it is equally important to assess our beliefs about what we want to create.

You're familiar with the concept of the self-fulfilling prophecy, right? Henry Ford once said, "Whether you believe you can or you believe you can't, you're right." He was pointing to the starring role that thinking plays in making things happen – or not.

The truth is, our thoughts and beliefs are the basis for our actions and behavior, which in turn produce our results. Long-held beliefs are a very powerful comfort zone. And as we have discussed, some comfort zones serve us and some do not.

What we believe determines how we behave, which in turn determines the results we achieve. Here's a simple example of how this process works.

Scenario #1: Joe is a salesman at a large technology company. He wants to develop a more strategic relationship with a key healthcare client, because he sees a need in healthcare that could be satisfied in part by some emerging technology he sells. Joe believes that he's too inexperienced to make C-level calls, so he continues to make calls with the I/T departments and never gets the attention of the business executives who would drive business innovation. So, Joe is still considered a "vender."

Scenario #2: Joe is a salesman at a large technology company. He wants to develop a more strategic relationship with a key healthcare client, because he sees a need in healthcare that could be satisfied in part by some emerging technology he sells. Joe believes that he's a thought leader with strong communication skills, so he begins to make sales calls to leaders of various business units. One business unit leader has also seen this need in his industry and engages Joe as a partner to collaborate with his unit on a new innovation initiative. As a result, Joe is becoming a trusted advisor.

Our beliefs are either our greatest saboteurs, or our greatest allies. If we believe we're going to fail, we behave accordingly and the outcome is predictable. For this reason, we must become conscious and intentional about which beliefs will serve our Bigger

Game, and which will sabotage it. And we must be willing to shed or shift beliefs that are not serving us.

In Scenario #1, Joe can assess whether his belief that he is too inexperienced is serving his Bigger Game. He must be conscious of this belief and assess whether or not it's true. What is underneath the belief? Perhaps, in fact, Joe lacks confidence and relevant industry information to initiate a compelling business conversation. In this case, he could invest in building on his abilities or identify an ally with industry expertise.

Let's say that Joe consciously assesses his technical ability and determines that in fact, it is an asset when leveraged with his understanding of the client's business. In this case, he shifts his belief and gains the confidence to make those business unit sales calls.

In either case, whether the belief was true or not, the important first step was for Joe to become conscious of the belief and assess it, without judgment, in service to his intention to develop a more strategic relationship.

If we believe we're going to succeed, our odds of succeeding are greatly improved (although, of course, there are no guarantees). Sometimes, believing that something will happen feels like an enormous leap of faith – such is nearly always true with a Bigger Game if it is indeed big enough. Even when our goal is considerably less lofty, though, there's no way of knowing for sure whether or not things will actually turn out the way we want them to. Therefore, we are almost always "making up" our beliefs with no basis in fact, so we might as well invent beliefs that actively promote success.

Clear intention supported by conscious, positive belief serves as the basis for bold action and also serves as a beacon of vision and hope whenever we hit a rough patch in the game. It helps us to maintain focus and resolve, and it inspires and rallies the people we lead. Clear intention is integral to our ability to lead others.

Emotionally intelligent leadership and the Bigger Game
Choosing where to put your attention, aligning your intention with your beliefs, assessing rather than voting, and Meet-Point-Dance... these are core competencies that will create successful Bigger

Games. They are also integral to emotionally intelligent leadership, or the inspired and inspiring, resonant leadership that calls forth the best in your colleagues and constituents alike.

The key competencies of emotionally intelligent leadership, as defined by Daniel Goleman, Annie McKee, and Richard Boyatzis in their best-selling book, *Primal Leadership*, are a useful context for the way Bigger Game players lead others. The two basic domains of emotionally intelligent leadership include personal competence and social competence. Personal competence has to do with how we perceive and manage ourselves. Do our thoughts and emotions have us by the throat (attention on self/voting)? Or are we aware that we are thinking and experiencing emotions so that we can choose how and when to respond? Are we assessing our own strengths and limits with clear eyes? Can we respond flexibly to what is needed in this moment (dance)? Are we confident? Optimistic? Clear in our intentions and beliefs? Authentic and honest?

The emotional intelligence domain of social competence includes social awareness and relationship management. Do we empathize with others' thoughts and emotions, taking an active interest in who they are and what they care about (meet)? Are we dedicated to serving others (responding to a hunger in the human field)? Are we inspiring and influential? Do we know how to develop others and lead them in a new direction (point)?

In *Primal Leadership*, the authors underscore the fact that emotions and states of mind are highly contagious, especially when they start with the leader. When people are inspired by and feel positive about their leader, they form stronger collaborations, accomplish more, and do it faster. That's what we want for you as a Bigger Game leader.

The focus of this chapter has been the context and skills associated with becoming a successful Bigger Game leader. However, this kind of leadership is all theoretical without *action*. The Bigger Game is a results-oriented success model, and successful results require bold action at every turn. That's where we're moving in the next chapter. Read on.

Summary

• A Bigger Game is by the people (collaboration) and for the people (the field served). Consequently, a player needs to become the kind of leader who calls forth the best in self and others.

• Human beings aim their attention in three general directions: self, other, and the field. Bigger Game leaders keep their attention mostly on the field (which includes self and other as part of the field).

• Intention – which comprises clear goals plus aligned beliefs – is an indispensable tool in a leader's kit.

• Meet-Point-Dance - we meet people where they are, point them where we want them to go, and dance with whatever comes up by meeting or pointing them again.

• Assess versus vote – assessing is discerning something, or the ability to see how things are going – and how I'm doing – from a neutral perspective. Voting, or overlaying judgment on assessment, clouds our clear vision by turning our attention from the field onto ourselves. A Bigger Game player's job is to constantly assess, without voting.

• Recovering to the field - Noticing and assessing our impact on others is an important element of the Meet-Point-Dance cycle. Sometimes, though, our impact will delight or dismay us in a way that pulls our attention from the field onto ourselves. When this happens, we need to notice the pull and consciously redirect our attention to the field. With practice, we can shorten recovery times dramatically.

• A Bigger Game player practices emotionally intelligent leadership by developing facility in self-awareness, self-management, social awareness (empathy), and relationship management.

Chapter 4
Twister! Bold Action and Assess

As we've said before, this book has a number of purposes: to reveal the Bigger Game player you already are, to help you find the Bigger Game that fires your soul, and, most importantly, to help you use Bigger Game playing to consciously design who you are becoming. The payoff of the latter is enormous: Playing a Bigger Game accelerates your acquisition of new competencies, leadership skills, and confidence. At the same time, you get to feed your soul's hunger, have a major impact on others, and experience personal success. All it takes is strategic bold action, and that's what we'll be addressing in this chapter.

In the last chapter, we laid out some core competencies to help you succeed with your Bigger Game. These competencies represent the "being" of a Bigger Game player, the infrastructure that supports both your personal growth and your achievements. Without the "doing" side of the model, however, leadership principles are nothing more than good ideas and a launching pad. For what? For bold action... the "doing" side of the model that transforms your game from concept to reality.

Webster's Dictionary defines *bold* as "intrepid, fearless before danger, requiring a courageous spirit." Now, we actually don't believe that there is such a thing as "fearlessness." If you are attempting to do something risky that you have never done before and the outcome matters to you, you are very likely to be at least a little scared of it. Therefore, we prefer the word *undaunted*, which means "taking action in the face of fear." The point is to go ahead and have the fear – don't wait until you feel fearless because you might wait forever – and then just do whatever it is that scares you.

In general, you aren't acting merely for the sake of action. (In fact, the pattern of constant busyness is actually a very common comfort zone.) Sometimes, though, you may need to do something – *anything!* – to blast out of particularly intransigent inertia. The bold action we're pointing to here is strategic, at least most of the time. Your action is informed by what your game needs – and what you need to be the best player you can possibly be. That's why this chapter centers on both Bold Action and Assess, the components of the Bigger Game that help you determine what's most important to do next.

Assess – constant course adjustments

In the last chapter, we addressed the difference between assessing – getting a clear, neutral read on what's happening so as to open up new possibilities – and voting, overlaying your judgments, preferences, and opinions over assessment in a way that clouds your vision and limits your options. "Assess" is also a key element of the Bigger Game Board. In this context, it has to do with knowing how your game is going and knowing how you are doing at any given moment. Because the truth is, things change.

Try this analogy on for size: Think of your Bigger Game as a transatlantic sailboat. You started in Boston and your destination/desired outcome is London. You've set your course and have plenty of provisions on board. So, you sail boldly out of the harbor and tack northeast to take advantage of the prevailing wind. And then the wind changes, so you have to adjust your course and tack southeast for a day or two. And then a storm blows you off course and you are exhausted from responding to storm conditions for the last 13 hours, so you reef your sails and take a long nap below. When you come up, you notice you've been blown many degrees north, so you need to tack southward until you're back on course. And you're monitoring the radio to ascertain where the storm is centered because it's well worth taking a detour in order to avoid those mountainous seas. You're still heading for London and doing fine, yet you must make constant course corrections in response to changing conditions and your personal needs for rest and replenishment.

Similarly, a Bigger Game evolves in response to the prevailing conditions in your world. And you evolve, too. What once constituted a bold action may now be yet another comfort zone that slows you down. New opportunities open up. Other doors slam shut. At this moment, you may need to pour it on or give it a rest. At every step in the process, it is essential to know where you are and the state of your game so that the next bold action can be predicated on what is needed now.

To assess involves telling yourself as much truth as you can, as clearly as you can see it. Getting your tendency to vote out of the way helps. Still, all human beings have blind spots, so it is often useful to solicit feedback from your allies on how you're doing and how the game is going – and the more, the better.

"Bold Action" and "Assess" sit side by side on the Game Board, one at the center and one to its left. Both are contextual, meaning that wherever else you may be on the Game Board, you need to have a hand in Bold Action and your eyes and brain on Assess at all times. When you're playing a Bigger Game, you are occupying at least three parts of the Game Board simultaneously. Remember the Twister game board analogy? You'd better get limber and agile – you'll need it!

Bold Action in every element

Bold Action is the center square of the Bigger Game Board because every other square requires boldness at some time, if not all the time. Any step you're taking on the Game Board usually requires some boldness.

For example, comfort zones require that you do a cost/benefit analysis of your routines and habits and then deliberately relinquish those that don't serve your game. Giving up smoking? Taking up an exercise regimen? Getting married? Getting divorced? Quitting your job? Transforming an "I can't" state of mind to "I can"? Leaving comfort zones often requires monumental leaps of action and thinking.

Awakening and exploring hunger are similarly bold. Most of us have been trained to assuage our hunger pangs with easy comforts. Allowing ourselves to probe deeply into the hunger of our souls requires that we look both inside ourselves and out into the world. We cannot know what we ache to change if we are not in touch with what is missing or needed. The bold action here includes reaching out – having deep conversations with our team or colleagues at work, volunteering in the community, watching the news, asking questions, extending our antennae. Looking inside requires the paradoxical boldness of getting quiet, reflecting, allowing our hunger pangs to gnaw at us without succumbing to the immediate but shallow gratification of distractions.

Finding your compelling purpose and naming your Bigger Game require bold action. Start with saying the name of your game out loud – and often – until it becomes real to you and others know what you're up to. In order for your compelling purpose to continue to resonate with its original power, you need to find ways to keep it alive. Conscious attention to your commitments may not seem as bold as venturing forth on a Greenpeace boat to save the whales, yet a resolute stand of "This must be – and it must be me" is the backbone of any Bigger Game, and, as such, is bold indeed.

Consider investment and sustainability. What are the attitudes and beliefs you need to cultivate? The holes in your expertise you need to fill with education and training? The health rituals you need to establish and maintain for the sake of your game? The space and equipment to support what you're up to? Bold actions at every turn. And how about allies? What bold actions are necessary to attract and serve co-players, expert resources, your clients and prospects, and other constituents? What actions do you need to take to establish and maintain these key relationships?

Wherever you find yourself on the Game Board, bold action – including the boldness of stillness – is what keeps you grounded, moving forward, and growing. To play a Bigger Game, you must move, you must be in action.... Otherwise, what you're playing is nothing more than a mind game.

Dare to know – don't worry if it's right

How do you know what your next move should be *and* where and how to make it? Bold action within the Bigger Game context can feel like stepping off a cliff into thin air, with no assurance that a net will appear beneath you. Many people are steeped in the comfort of competence and the principle of "look before you leap." When they are standing on the edge of the cliff, it is hugely tempting to step back, turn around, and retreat to competence and its predictable outcomes. For these people, it requires incredible boldness to take action without knowing in advance whether or not it will work.

Here's what makes the decision-making process a little easier. You may not know what your next move should be, but your compelling purpose knows and your Bigger Game knows. If you keep your attention on the field and on your own hunger, your Bigger Game will tell you what to do. It still won't deliver any guarantees of effectiveness, but that doesn't really matter in the larger scheme of things. There are very few actions you can take that are actually fatal. When something doesn't work, you can try something else. That's why we couple "dare to know" (let your Bigger Game decide your next move for you) with "don't worry if it's right" (don't be attached to any particular outcome). Therefore, if you can give yourself to the mandates of your game and let go of the need to get it right, you are then free to respond to your game, move, recover, respond, move, and recover again. Your bold action becomes a fluid dance in which you lead and you are led.

Embrace failing

Every one of us has experienced the joy of demonstrating our own splendid competence. This is not the joy that Bigger Game players are shooting for, however. When we are doing what we already know how to do, we may be effective and accomplish a great deal, but we don't grow ourselves. Exponential personal development happens only when we're taking on new challenges, and doing what we've never done before almost always includes failing at least some of the time. Bigger Game players, therefore, learn to embrace failing for the gifts of learning it delivers. We don't have to fall in love with failing (though we might); rather, we need to build an appetite for taking bold actions that are risky, knowing that failing is inevitable and builds our capacity like nothing else on earth.

As the German nihilist philosopher Frederich Nietzsche once said, "That which does not kill us makes us stronger." In fact, very few of the bold actions associated with playing a Bigger Game pose any kind of threat to your actual survival. No matter how you might embarrass yourself, there is always a warm bed and a good meal to look forward to at the other end of bold action. A large part of capacity building is expanding your willingness to fail and then failing bigger, knowing that the consequences simply aren't all that bad.

Besides, failing and recovering is absolutely the best way to learn anything new and embody it.

Feel the fear, do it anyway... and watch the fear disappear
It is impossible for fear and bold action to coexist in the same moment. When you're afraid to do something, the moment you step into action is the moment that particular fear begins to become a thing of your past.

In January 2006, Caroline MacNeill Hall was visiting Queenstown, New Zealand, the place where bungee-jumping was invented a few decades back. She had been contemplating the possibility of making a jump on and off during the week prior to the visit – and with each thought of it, her stomach had twisted and her throat had closed up a bit. When at last she found herself beneath the bridge, gazing up at each jumper poised 200 feet above the rushing blue river, her mouth got dry and her heartbeat picked up speed. It would be so easy not to do this. After all, there were no other grandmothers up there. Ultimately, though, Caroline felt she couldn't pass up such a great opportunity to be afraid of something and do it anyway. Truth is, though, the moment she committed to make the jump – when "maybe" became "will" – most of her fear simply vanished. She stepped onto the tiny platform over the river, looked at the water, the sky, and the trees, felt the sensation one experiences as a roller coaster is suspended right at the top of a climb, and swan-dived joyfully off the platform. What was initially scary became exhilarating. This is often true. And even though skydiving had always been just about the scariest thing she could think of, three days after bungee-jumping, Caroline jumped out of an airplane at 13,000 feet – and found it delightful. It can be astonishing how quickly something that scares us becomes a new comfort zone with a little practice.

A key element of this dynamic is that moving into a risk requires that you take your attention off of yourself and direct it out to the field. Fear exists primarily when you are listening mostly to your own thinking – especially your thoughts about you. Once you are focused out there, the fear mostly dissipates, your perspective broadens to include the whole field, and you become nimble, resourceful, and resilient.

In his book *The Scottish Himalayan Expedition*, W.H. Murray asserted, "Until one is committed, there is hesitancy, the chance to draw back, always ineffectiveness. Concerning all acts of initiative and creation, there is one elementary truth, the ignorance of which kills countless ideas and splendid plans: that the moment one definitely commits oneself, then Providence moves, too. All sorts of things occur to help one that would never otherwise have occurred. A whole stream of events issues from the decision, raising in one's favor all manner of unforeseen incidents and meetings and material assistance, which no man could have dreamt would come his way. I learned a deep respect for one of [the German philosopher] Goethe's couplets: 'Whatever you can do, or dream you can, begin it. Boldness has genius, power, and magic in it.'"

In our experience, once you commit to step into bold action, synchronicity flows in at about the same proportion as fear wanes – and the magic kicks in.

Some comfort zones have a high cost to your game and need to be abandoned. Other comfort zones are useful for Bigger Game players to cultivate. One of the latter is to make a practice of doing things that scare and thrill you – from taking leadership on your company's cornerstone project to bungee-jumping to public speaking to cold-calling a big client to grabbing the microphone in a karaoke bar. As you take bold action to conquer the fear associated with each of these activities, you eventually discover that a) not much scares you anymore; and b) even when it does scare you, you know that you'll emerge stronger on the other side because you've done it so many times before. Bottom line: Meeting the gulp with action is a key characteristic of seasoned Bigger Game players.

Compelling purpose is the pull to action

A comfort zone such as taking on a stretch challenge every day certainly provides a push to action. Sometimes, though, it can be awfully tempting to resist the push, find an excuse, and go do something else that feels equally urgent at the moment (such as returning e-mail). As coaches, we have noticed that the human animal comes equipped with an exceedingly limited supply of self-discipline, and we consume enormous energy whenever we tap into that limited resource.

The cool thing about playing a Bigger Game is that bold action is born of compelling purpose. When the change you want to create absolutely must happen, your compelling purpose pulls you forward as surely as a team of horses pulls a carriage toward the barn when oats are waiting. You don't have to exercise self-discipline. You don't have to try. You don't have to work hard. Bigger Game players who are in touch with their purpose are pulled into a bold move, assess where they are, and then are led to the next step. So the challenge is not to force yourself to make a move; rather, it is to find the compelling purpose – the good enough reason – that gives you no choice but to move boldly toward the future you yearn to create.

And finding your compelling purpose and the name of your Bigger Game is the focus of the next section – and the heart – of this book.

Summary

- Bold Action represents the "doing" side of the Bigger Game Board that transforms the name of your game into something real in your world.

- To play a Bigger Game, you must be in action.... Otherwise, what you're playing is a mind game.

- Bold Action and Assess are both context elements for the model, meaning they are always happening, no matter what other element you may be occupying simultaneously. Twister!

- Assessment is iterative. The field changes from moment to moment and you do, too. So you need to check regularly to determine where you are in order to decide where to go next.

- Bold action is bold because it entails doing something new, risky, and at least a little bit scary. These are the elements that create learning and grow human beings.

- Bold action involves failing, at least some of the time. Bigger Game players must cultivate an appetite (or at least a tolerance) for failing for the sake of the learning it engenders.

- Fear precedes action; it does not coexist with it. Once you move into action around something that scares you, the fear dissipates – and your capacity has grown.

- Developing the comfort zone of doing things that scare and thrill you is a useful habit for Bigger Game players.

- It requires enormous self-discipline to make yourself do something you aren't inclined to do, and human beings have a limited capacity for discipline. Fortunately, when you are compelled enough, it pulls you into action so you no longer have to push yourself. In a very real sense, Bigger Game players are led.

Section Two
How Do I Find My Bigger Game?

The chapters just ahead are your invitation to connect with your soul hunger, resonating purpose, and drive that will elicit your best, ask for everything you have, and grow you as you identify the contribution your world wants from you.

One evening, an old Cherokee warrior told his grandson about a battle that goes on inside all human beings. He said, "My son, the battle is between the two wolves that live inside us all. One wolf is Evil. It is anger, envy, jealousy, sorrow, regret, greed, arrogance, self-pity, guilt, resentment, inferiority, lies, false pride, superiority, and ego. The other wolf is Good. It is joy, peace, love, hope, serenity, humility, kindness, benevolence, empathy, generosity, truth, compassion, and faith." The grandson thought about this for a minute and then asked his grandfather: "Which wolf wins the battle?" The old Cherokee replied, "Whichever wolf you feed."

Human nature incorporates both wolves. And, like the boy in the story above, we get to choose which side we're going to nourish. Consider:

Bad Wolf:
• Almost all human beings, from time to time, tell lies, cheat, slack off, blame others, and develop habits and routines that serve no one.
• Human beings move rapidly to blame in order to justify their view of themselves.
• Human beings dull their hunger for meaning with easy comforts and distractions.
• Human beings often judge others unfavorably for making the same mistakes they make themselves.
• Human beings can be delighted at a friend's success and at the same time feel disappointed and envious.
• Human beings fail to respect the beauty that nature offers and are destroying Planet Earth by treating it as a personal plaything.
• Human beings are selfish, greedy, and think only of themselves.

Good Wolf:
• Human beings have a sense of what is appropriate and "right," an inner knowing that reflects their true essence. Some of us live according to that essence, some betray it, while most of us flicker back and forth.
• Human beings are capable of great generosity in the face of tremendous stress and hardship.
• Human beings hunger for meaning in their lives.
• Human beings are artists who create beauty that moves the soul.
• Human beings routinely exhibit the greatest love the world has ever known.

Bigger Game players routinely feed the good wolf – the best part of their natures. They do it not because they are goody-goodies or marvels of self-discipline, but rather because they have a good enough reason, their compelling purpose. The fact is, once you know your compelling purpose and the name of your Bigger Game, they pull you along and become the making of you. You actually don't have to try, and the work isn't hard so much as it is an exhilarating, focused stretch. Once your game has you in its thrall, you're in flow and you're usually having more fun than you ever had before.

For this to happen, of course, a player has to have a compelling purpose – one that feeds the soul while it serves the field. The lucky ones among us already know what our purpose is. Some exceptionally fortunate people are practically born knowing the difference they're eager to make. For the rest of us, though, finding the purpose that fires our souls, vibrates our bellies, and moves our feet requires focus, commitment, trial and error, and the uncomfortable ambiguity of not knowing.

The discomfort of not knowing, in fact, is what knocks most potential Bigger Game players off the Game Board before they've even begun. And that's a shame and a waste, because every human being has a unique contribution to make, a song to sing that is theirs alone for the sake of the higher good. And if you die without making your mark or singing your song, it is your loss and the world's.

For most people, the exploration process – multiple forays into the "fog" of the unknown – is the most challenging part of playing a Bigger Game. That's why this section of the book is so important for all of you who have not already named your games. The section lays out a step-by-step process – one that often runs counter to how our culture has trained us to think and behave – for finding the Bigger Game that will thrill you and grow you as it transforms your corner of the world.

It's not as if the exploration process stops there, of course. The world changes. You change. You accomplish what you set out to do and it's done. What's next? How do you heed the next call, find the next iteration of your compelling purpose, your "new and improved" Bigger Game?

Whether you have already named a game, are bored and looking for more richness and meaning in your life, used to be a player and lost it somewhere along the way, or fall somewhere in between, these chapters are essential reading. Staying in the exploration process is absolutely integral to working the Bigger Game Board from this day forward for the rest of your life.

Remember, you don't have to have a Bigger Game to play on the Bigger Game Board. The moment you decide you want to make a significant contribution and commit to rousing and exploring your hunger, you've already taken the field. This section is all about showing you how to find your Bigger Game and allowing your Bigger Game to find you. And it's about staying hungry.

Chapter 5
Leaving Comfort Zones: Saying Good-Bye to Business as Usual

Comfortable: "affording or enjoying contentment or security, encourages complacency; absence of anything likely to cause physical or mental discomfort"
Complacency: "self-satisfaction accompanied by unawareness of actual dangers or deficiencies" (*Webster's Dictionary*)

The good news: comfort zones serve us
Human beings are creatures of habit, and that is good news. The average adult doesn't wake up in the morning, feel hunger pangs, and wander around the house gnawing on the bedpost, licking the sink, or tearing into the sock drawer in a frustrating quest for nourishment. Rather, we have learned to head straight for the fridge and the warm embrace of Mr. Coffee. Nor do we have to start from scratch every time we take a shower, tie our shoes, drive to work,

run a meeting, order sushi, and turn off the lights. Thank goodness we have learned the thinking and action associated with each of these activities so that they require no thought, discipline, or will-power at all. We just do them automatically.

These habits constitute some of our "comfort zones." Comfort zones include those habits and routine ways of thinking, behaving, and feeling that we do automatically, without having to think. At their best, comfort zones make our lives infinitely easier by creating safety, saving time, and freeing up our energy and attention for other things.

The bad news: comfort zones thwart us

Now, here's the bad news: Human beings are creatures of habit. We have developed all these comfort zones that keep us safe and comfortable and efficient – hurray! And yet, we are at our best – our most creative and inspired and powerful – when we are going after something we've never done before and don't know how to do. The moment discomfort rushes in to fill the gap between what we want and the limit of our competence is the very moment that human growth begins. It's also the moment when our comfort zones exert a ferocious tug on us – a pull back to the status quo where we are competent and safe.

Here are some other ways of saying "comfort zone." Business as usual. Same old, same old. Just the way things are. At their worst, comfort zones anesthetize and swaddle us so that we miss experiencing the richness, growth, and meaning that characterize a human life fully lived.

Everybody has comfort zones – and lots of them. Developing routines and habits is a normal and natural tendency. Some of our comfort zones serve us. Other comfort zones keep us stuck in mediocrity. Still others threaten our health, well-being, and sense of accomplishment. All comfort zones have some kind of benefit and some kind of cost attached to them. Even the most useful of our comfort zones costs us something. The point for Bigger Game players to remember is that comfort zones represent what you already know, and playing a Bigger Game requires that you step into the unknown. This means you need to leave the comfort zones that don't serve you. And to leave them, you need to know that you have them. That's why identifying and examining your comfort zones is one of the most important practices a Bigger Game player can establish.

Kinds of comfort zones

Comfort zones come in two basic varieties: habits of action and habits of thinking. Habits of action range from brushing your teeth each morning to pumping iron three times a week to grabbing a latte every time you pass a Starbucks. From meditating each morning for an hour... to zoning out in front of the TV most every evening. From doing your employees' assignments for them with a martyred sigh... to coaching them to autonomy. You get the picture – some comfort zones of action serve us and some don't.

The same holds true for our habits of thinking. They range from "I'm not good enough" to "There's nothing I can't do" and everything in between. From "Why should I stick my neck out?" to "I don't know how, so I won't" to "Failing demonstrates courage, so I'm gonna go for it!" Again, the fact that we have comfort zones is neither good nor bad; it's just a fact. It's also a fact that some habits of thought are useful to us, and some are not.

As Bigger Game players, we're not looking to get rid of our comfort zones by any means. Rather, we need to constantly notice that we have comfort zones of action and thought – and assess whether they serve our game and us.

You must have noticed by now that "comfort" in this context includes familiarity as much as it does pleasure. For example, that leaden feeling in your stomach after you inhale your fast-food lunch may not be pleasant, but it sure is familiar. In fact, many of our psychological comfort zones create sovereign nations of chronic anxiety, righteousness, insecurity, defensiveness, and various other forms of self-sabotage.

How did this kind of thinking get to be a habit in the first place? It's probably true that sometime in the past, we learned to be really careful with matches so we wouldn't get burned. And we learned that other risks were just as dangerous and we shouldn't take them either. The irony is that risk aversion is the kind of comfort zone that keeps us mired in a swamp of routine and limits our growth. It's ironic, isn't it? We develop comfort zones in the first place to keep ourselves safe and happy, yet over time, these habits actually devolve us to a state of boredom and complacency.

There are four major types of comfort zones that can stop Bigger Game players before they get on the Game Board. The first is the *habit zone*. Examples? Managing tasks instead of people, doing it all yourself instead of delegating, working late too often, and neglecting self-care. Then we have the *indulgence zone*, which includes things like eating junk food, smoking cigarettes, drinking alcohol to excess, skimming through catalogs and magazines as you eat, and complaining. Next comes the *ego safety zone*, where habits include defending your self-image, avoiding anger or sadness, acting out of self-righteousness, and holding back what you're thinking for fear of losing your job, being seen as inadequate or wrong, being disliked, and/or being embarrassed. And finally, we come to the *pain avoidance zone*, where we might find ourselves avoiding performance reviews, avoiding challenging encounters, avoiding being wrong at all costs, delaying dental and medical appointments, littering, or taking the elevator instead of the stairs.

Here's another place to look for comfort zones: What are the roles you habitually play in your life? Are you the caretaker (Hi, Mom!) ensuring that everyone else is safe and fed and wearing a sweater? Are you the expert who always has the answer, no matter what the question? Or the general, who is forever issuing orders and instructions? The free spirit who does whatever he wants whenever he wants? The martyr? ("Well then," said the Little Red Hen, "if you won't help, I'll just do it myself!") Notice the roles that you gravitate toward in your life. Which serve you? Which hold you back? And how do you need to expand your repertoire?

Here's yet another place to look for comfort zones. Where in your life are you the most capable and competent? What would people say your strengths are? For what qualities do you consistently achieve success and receive acknowledgment? What do you always say yes to simply because you're good at it, whether or not you have time or actually want to do it? Our strengths and competencies are often the biggest comfort zones of all – and the hardest to leave.

And finally, here are some habits of thought or belief that have cost many their Bigger Game:

• It's too hard.
• It must be perfect or I don't want to do it.
• I can do it all myself.
• I know I'm right.
• I don't wanna and you can't make me.
• I don't have enough time.
• I don't know how.
• I can't.
• I need a guarantee first.

Any of the above sound familiar? Well yeah, now that you think about it. And that's just the thing – we don't think about our comfort zones much. They are largely unconscious, unexamined, and often damned near invisible ways of thinking and acting. That's what makes them so insidious.

Going unconscious

Let's delve a little deeper into the anatomy of a comfort zone. In his book *Deep Survival* author Laurence Gonzales reports that we humans learn to navigate the world via emotional bookmarks, or learned habits of feeling and thinking. For example, let's say a dog bit Jimmy when he was four. His response was pain and fear. Now he is 24, and every time he sees a dog, he still experiences pain and fear. Then there's Sally, who, in the third grade, ran to victory in the 100-yard dash to the cheers of all the teachers and parents. This experience created a delicious emotional experience for Sally; that's why she runs marathons as an adult.

Emotional bookmarks reactivate the thoughts and feelings associated with a specific circumstance every time a similar circumstance occurs. Using emotional bookmarks as building blocks, we then construct personal mental models that help us filter the barrage of information that assails us 24/7 so that we see only what we expect to see, just when we expect to see it. Our mental models create self-fulfilling prophecies that support our personal construct of the status quo and all our routines therein. "Every model of the world comes with its own underlying assumptions based on experience, memories, secondary emotions, and emotional bookmarks," says Gonzales, "all of which influence what we expect to happen and what we plan to do about it."

Actually, most of the time precious little planning is required. In fact, a growing body of research suggests that a staggering 95% of what we human beings do occurs without any conscious thought at all. Joseph LeDoux, a neuroscientist, writes, "Unconscious operations of the brain is... the rule rather than the exception throughout the evolutionary history of the animal kingdom and includes almost everything the brain does."

In other words, human beings are "hard-wired" to operate on automatic pilot – in comfort zones – unless there is a compelling reason for a course correction. It is normal and natural for us to operate out of habit. When this is happening – which is most of the time – we are in our comfort zones, those cozy, familiar nests where we don't have to think. We are competent, capable, comfortable, and we really know our way around. It's business as usual, and the living is, if not always easy, at least predictable.

Pleasure vs. meaning

For eons, human beings have been genetically programmed to 1) seek pleasure, 2) avoid pain, and 3) conserve energy. Our at-all-costs pursuit of quick and easy pleasure is the major comfort zone in our full, rich lives, according to Drs. Douglas Lisle and Alan Goldhamer, authors of *The Pleasure Trap: Mastering the Hidden Force That Undermines Health and Happiness.*

They are not alone in their assertion that pleasure without meaning is ultimately empty. That's also the central premise of Mihaly Csikszentmihalyi's groundbreaking book *Flow: The Psychology of Optimal Experience.* Says Csikszentmihalyi, "Pleasure is the feeling of contentment that one achieves whenever... expectations set by biological programs or by social conditioning have been met... Resting in the evening while passively absorbing information from the media, with alcohol or drugs to dull the mind overexcited by the demands of work, is pleasantly relaxing... Pleasure is an important component of the quality of life, but by itself does not bring happiness... It provides restorative homeostatic experiences that return consciousness to order after the needs of the body intrude. But [it does] not produce psychological growth."

What *does* produce psychological growth is the challenge of the unknown, which pulls us right out of the homeostasis of our comfort zones into far less familiar territory. Given that we are creatures of habit, most people don't make a practice of volunteering for this kind of discomfort. But that's exactly what Bigger Game players are called to do – and do routinely. Stepping out of comfort zones by saying good-bye to business as usual is the first rule of the game. And the result is worth the discomfort – for the Game itself and, more important, for you, the player.

The good enough reason
The Comfort Zone element of the Bigger Game Board is based on a number of assertions:

1) Playing a Bigger Game requires you to do what you've never done before, to enter a place where the learning curve is steep. (That's part of what makes it a Bigger Game instead of just a big game.)
2) Doing what you don't know how to do requires that you leave behind habits of thinking and action that don't serve the game, and that you be willing to endure the discomfort of what's challenging and unfamiliar.

And why would you deliberately choose discomfort when your favorite show is on and the remote control unit is at hand? Here's why: There is something different you want to see in your world that is setting you on fire and making your heart race. This is your Bigger Game. It must happen, and you are the go-to person for it, no question about it. It takes a very good reason indeed to pull you out of the zone of habit onto the field of play, and that reason is a purpose so compelling that you simply can't say no.

The other good enough reason: who you're becoming

Foundational to the Bigger Game is the premise that playing a Bigger Game designs who you are becoming. A life lived within your comfort zones is pleasant at best and dead at worst. When you don't venture beyond the boundaries of your comfort zones, you don't grow and you aren't fulfilled. Ask yourself questions like these: "Who do you want to become?" "Is that a compelling enough reason to leave your comfort zones?"

So, here are a few more comfort zone assertions:

3) A fulfilling life requires meaning and growth. Tackling challenges head-on is a great way to grow.
4) When we leave the familiar to learn and do what's new and build our capacity, we automatically develop new, higher-level comfort zones because that's just what we humans do. This means that when we grow bigger, the game has to grow too, so that it's still big enough for the new us. This process, not incidentally, is extremely fun.
5) The more we examine and move out of comfort zones that don't serve us, the easier it becomes – and the more we grow.

In order to be a Bigger Game player, then, we need to be brave and scrupulous about identifying our comfort zones, examining them, eradicating the ones that don't serve the game, and creating new ones that do. Daunting? Well, sure. But doable.

The Bigger Game asks you to examine your particular comfort zones and explore the costs and benefits of each with respect to who you want to become and the impact you want to have. By the way, this means looking at all of your comfort zones, even the "good" ones. By choosing the comfort zones you want to move out of, those you want to keep, and new ones you want to cultivate, you are choosing to stretch toward a new personal best. And when you're stretching toward a new personal best in service of something that you care deeply about – your Bigger Game – the payoff is your big life *and* your big thumbprint on the world.

Making blind spots visible
Now, there is one major challenge in any effort to identify your comfort zones. Here it is: We have gaping blind spots around our comfort zones because they are so familiar to us; consequently, they can be very hard to spot. And if we don't recognize them and choose what to do with them, they tend to make our decisions for us. The fact is that unexamined comfort zones run our lives.

Becoming an "outsider" – the strategic approach
You want to become an expert at knowing when you're in a comfort zone, noticing whether or not it serves you, and choosing to blast out when it doesn't. Here's a strategic approach:

1) Apply what you've learned so far about comfort zones to identify yours, both those that serve and those that don't.
2) Determine the cost and benefit of living in each comfort zone so you can choose which ones support you and your game, which don't, and what's missing.
3) Get conscious about when you're in a comfort zone and decide whether or not you want to stay there. (Tapping into your good enough reason – your compelling purpose – really helps here.) Frequently choose to venture outside for no good reason, just to become adept at becoming an "outsider."
4) Develop strategies for moving beyond particularly damaging or high-cost comfort zones.
5) Thinking is good, but it's less than half the equation. Take bold actions in examining and leaving your comfort zones whenever possible.
6) Engage allies to help you identify those comfort zones that you just can't see.

Leaving the nest: the learning steps
Recognizing and examining comfort zones is one thing. Changing them is another matter. For those who choose to play a Bigger

Game – which requires that you leave highly valued comfort zones – it is helpful to put some context around how personal growth and change actually occur. The model below represents the different stages we pass through as we learn to embody new skills and abilities.

The Learning Steps

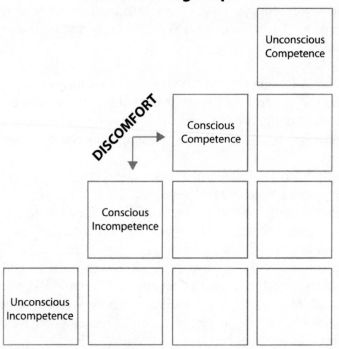

1) Unconscious Incompetence: We don't know what we don't know, a.k.a. "ignorance is bliss."
2) Conscious Incompetence: We know what we don't know and we desperately want to know it! This is the most uncomfortable phase of learning and, unfortunately, it is a phase we don't get to skip.
3) Conscious Competence: We know what we know, but we have to think about it because we don't yet have it in our bones.
4) Unconscious Competence: We've got the new learning in our bones. And voila, a new comfort zone is born!

Each of the steps in the model represents a different level of comfort. You'll notice that comfort zones appear in steps 1 and 4, where unconsciousness rules. Conscious competence is slightly uncomfortable, and conscious incompetence... well... it would be fabulous to skip this stage altogether. However, the more we engage in the growth process, knowing that conscious incompetence is an inevitable part of the learning cycle, the more we can celebrate our willingness to step into the unknown for the sake of what matters to us.

The point here is that learning and growth require leaving what we already know – our comfort zones. Our Bigger Game demands that we do it, and it gives us a good enough reason to endure whatever discomfort may follow. And after you practice the pattern of leaving what's comfortable over time, this pattern, too, becomes a comfort zone – and one with major benefits for your Bigger Game!

More good news: the hard stuff becomes habit
Those who routinely choose discomfort increase their agility, build their capacity to operate effectively amidst ambiguity, and have the greatest impact. What's more, they develop new comfort zones: What once was challenging soon becomes business as usual. So here's the most important competency to be building: the ability to consciously transform what is hard and uncomfortable into a new habit. This means converting that gulpy energy into action until the new behavior itself becomes routine. Once this behavior becomes a comfort zone, we can then seek out the next comfort zone to step away from or to cultivate – always, of course, in service of our Bigger Game.

Comfort zones are marvelous tools when you develop good ones... and we develop them really fast. In their book *The Power of Full Engagement* Jim Loehr and Tony Schwartz point out that human beings have a limited resource of self-discipline and willpower for acting and thinking consciously. However, once you cultivate a habit (they call it a "ritual") regularly for a relatively short time, you no longer have to think about it because automatic pilot kicks in. In this way, you can develop comfort zones that truly serve you and your Bigger Game.

"In contrast to will and discipline, which require pushing your-self to a particular behavior, a 'ritual' (habit) pulls at you," say Loehr and Schwartz in their book. "Positive rituals are powerful on three levels. They help us to ensure that we efficiently manage energy in the service of whatever mission we are on. They reduce the need to rely on our limited conscious will and discipline to take action. And finally, rituals are a powerful means by which to translate our values and priorities into action – to embody what matters most to us in our everyday behaviors."

Even so, beware! Beware! However elegantly they serve us, the comfort zones of rituals breed unconsciousness, and unconsciousness has a high cost to Bigger Games. So keep examining them. Keep consciously choosing your life.

The most fun you'll ever have

A final note: If this chapter makes it seem that leaving comfort zones in service of your Bigger Game is a grim slog, let us correct that impression here and now. Leaving comfort zones – and learning all the new ways you can step up to what matters most – is seriously delightful. The pleasure of channel surfing doesn't come remotely close to the fulfillment of discovering what you're made of and seeing what you're capable of doing.

Enjoyment appears when you're playing a Bigger Game. You can count on that.

Summary

- Operating through habit and pursuing comfort are natural, normal human tendencies. We are pleasure-seeking organisms, and research shows that up to 95% of what we do is on automatic pilot, without conscious thought.

- Some comfort zones serve us and are useful. Other comfort zones numb us out, stymie our growth, and engender atrophy. In both cases, unexamined comfort zones run our lives.

- A Bigger Game, by definition, calls us to do what we have never done before and don't know how to do. It requires that we experience conscious incompetence, which is very uncomfortable.

- We humans have a limited supply of will and discipline to blast through our comfort zones and confront the status quo. We have to have a good enough reason. That would be your compelling purpose and your Bigger Game.

- To transform a comfort zone requires that we examine it, name it, identify the cost associated with it, and develop strategies to lose it or love it.

- New comfort zones emerge naturally in the course of playing a Bigger Game as we gain unconscious competence in new skills and grow ourselves. For your Bigger Game to stay big enough, it must grow and evolve right along with you.

Chapter 6
The Hunger,
a.k.a. Turning Up the "Wanter"

This chapter is about the value of being hungry – and staying hungry – in the pursuit of your Bigger Game. Hunger is perhaps the most essential component of the Bigger Game Board.

As you know, it takes a good enough reason, your compelling purpose, to pull you out of comfort zones toward the Bigger Game you are committed to play, personally or as part of a team. In order for a compelling purpose to exert that order of pull on you, it can't be just words on paper; it must set you on fire with how much your soul craves it. Your compelling purpose is, in fact, a product of hunger for what you want to create in your world. The hunger of your heart and soul is the driving force that compels you to action and keeps you moving, even when you and your co-players want to stop. So, as a Bigger Game player, the hungrier you are – and the more attuned you are to your hunger – the better.

Back in 1976, there was a movie called *Stay Hungry*. Great title. It starred Arnold Schwarzenegger pretty much as himself, an ambitious young bodybuilder from a tiny village in Austria. Arnold Schwarzenegger was fiercely hungry – hungry to become the best bodybuilder in the world, hungry to become a movie star. As he continued to stay hungry and refused to settle, he noticed not only what he wanted for himself, but also what he wanted for his adopted country. His personal hunger intersected with the hunger he perceived in the field, and he rose to the challenge by running for office. At the time of this writing, Arnold Schwarzenegger is the governor of California. Say what you want about the "Governator"; you have to respect a guy who has already reached the pinnacle of his profession and goes into public service to make a contribution.

The point is that allowing yourself to stay hungry – resisting the urge to distract yourself from the discomfort of unfulfilled longing – is the very foundation of a Bigger Game. In fact, without hunger, a Bigger Game is impossible.

The architecture of hunger

Physical hunger. You know how it feels. Your stomach is empty and growling. Your mouth salivates at the slightest scent of food. You feel a little lightheaded. You would kill for a burger. No matter what is happening around you, you can think of little else but "I want *food*. Now!"

This set of uncomfortable sensations triggers the amygdala, or the primitive reptilian brain at the base of the human skull charged with ensuring our physical survival. The amygdala is not the part of the brain that writes sonnets or thinks up cool ways to win the Nobel Prize. No, the amygdala is charged with instructing us to fight, flee, and feed. A million years ago, the amygdala used to say, "Hungry? Mastodon. Go!" Nowadays, the amygdala says, "Hungry? Golden Arches. Go!"

Meanwhile, our higher intelligence is protesting feebly: "Hold your horses, there. You're hungry because you're committed to drop a few pounds to stave off heart disease; a month from now, you'll be able to eat more of what you want." But we're not listening. The reason so many diets fail is that hunger feels so urgent that it demands satisfaction *right now*. Consequently, if there's no decent nourishment at hand, we feed our hunger with empty calories that don't truly nourish us.

Our spiritual and emotional hunger has roughly the same architecture as our physical hunger. We experience emptiness, a yearning to express ourselves fully, to make a difference in our worlds and have meaningful lives. Although there is less drooling involved, this form of wanting can be just as uncomfortable as physical starvation. And all too often, we are quick to sate it with the empty calories of consumerism and the comfort zones of busyness and entertainment when what we *really* want is the nourishment of purpose and meaning.

Maslow weighs in

Back in the early 1940s, psychologist Abraham Maslow defined the human hunger for meaning as the need for self-actualization, which topped his famous pyramid of human development. Maslow posited that human beings evolve according to a hierarchy of needs. Once the needs of each level are met, we hunger to fulfill the next level.

The bottom four levels of Maslow's Pyramid center around survival needs – for physical sustenance, safety, belonging, and respect. Maslow referred to these as "deficit needs"; if they aren't met, we spend our lives trying to fill the hole. Only after survival is handled can we ascend to the top of the pyramid, to the need for "self-actualization." This is the stage in which we yearn to apply our gifts and stretch ourselves in order to have an impact on what matters to us. Self-actualization involves becoming the best we can be and doing the most we possibly can with it. At the pinnacle of self-actualization is transcendence, or the drive to help others find fulfillment.

Once survival is assured, then, all human beings share this generic hunger to be used in the service of something bigger than us. Unfortunately, though, many of us get stalled in habitual survival-level thinking without ever making it to the top of Maslow's human development heap. In our consumer-oriented society, it's easy to convince ourselves that our very survival hinges on acquiring a late-model SUV or a plasma TV set. We keep ourselves busy earning the money to acquire these possessions and then get distracted by our many toys once we have them – more fast-food satiety in the comfort zone.

We're not saying that possessions are bad – not at all. We *are* saying that many of the comfort zones that originally were survival-oriented now have the effect of anesthetizing us so that we can't feel our deep, resonant hunger for purpose, meaning, and contribution. And we won't have a Bigger Game until we wake up and learn to let ourselves yearn – and yearn until it growls.

Comfort zones that kill our appetite for meaning

Two-year-olds know exactly what they want, and they aren't shy about demanding it. If they don't get it straightaway, they shriek, turn red, and pound the floor. Yes, that was once you and me. Our parents thought us uncivilized (true), and taught us to slam down the lid on our raw cravings. That was so frustrating, of course, that it was easier to stop wanting than to want something so badly and have to stifle it.

So, we learned that wanting things is selfish and that expressing what we want is uncouth. There are lots of other, related reasons why we have allowed our "wanters" to atrophy. For example, if we don't think we can get something, we don't want to risk disappointment, so it's better not to want. If we don't think we're capable of doing whatever it is we want to do, it's better not to want. If our hunger is too big – how can just one person like me change the world? It's better not to want.

And when we get practiced at dialing down our hunger, we often lose touch with what we want – and then experience the leaden angst of not knowing. We compare ourselves to others who are charged up about the big things they're doing, and we feel small and guilty by comparison. There's an old story that when each of us arrives at the Pearly Gates of Heaven, St. Peter will ask us to account for how we used our God-given gifts before he'll let us enter. Just the thought of how we're squandering our "potential" can make us crawl into bed and pull the covers over our heads. It's better to stay so busy that we don't have to think about that emptiness. It's better not to want. Or so we tell ourselves.

Perhaps most insidious of all, most of us don't really have to want anything. We're physically comfortable and there are people who love us. When we get bored or anxious or wondering if this is all there is to life, there is always the next e-mail to return, car to buy, show to watch, or dog to wash. Oh yes, hunger insinuates itself into our consciousness every now and then, but we know how to muffle its voice before it becomes a shout.

It is actually possible to live out an entire life this way? Many people do.

The "wanter"

Imagine that you have a dial – about the size of a kitchen timer – in your solar plexus where your ribs meet in the middle. This dial is your "wanter." It has settings from 1-10. Many of us keep the dial set around 2 or 3 – we do experience the odd hunger pang of the soul, but we tend to distract ourselves from it in short order.

Now, imagine turning your wanter up to 6. You slow down. You not only notice what you want, but you want it with an unfamiliar intensity. If you still don't know what you want, you let yourself sit in the question without distracting yourself from the discomfort of not knowing.

How about cranking your wanter up to 8? This is getting really uncomfortable. If you know what you want, you're wondering how you can make it happen – the "how" question makes you suffer and want to think about something else. And yet, the aliveness and resonance of your hunger are palpable. Then again, if you still don't know what you want, the ambiguity of not knowing weighs on you. Everything in you begs you to dial your wanter back down to your numb old comfort zone. And as a Bigger Game player, everything in you must resist because there is a huge payoff in letting yourself want.

It seems pretty obvious, but the more you allow yourself to want, the more you *do* want – and the more you accomplish in the world. Let's say Mother Theresa only wanted to save a single starving baby in India. So she did that... and she was done. That's a worthy contribution, of course. But think about it. Through her ferocious hunger to save *all* children, Mother Theresa made an incalculable difference in the world. Did she know how she was going to save so many before she began? Of course not. No script exists for what has never been done before. Nor did her skill set suggest that she was equipped to have an impact of that magnitude. But Mother Theresa started with "I want." And it grew into "I will." And then to "I can." And finally to "I did."

Remember, "Can I?" will stop you cold. You don't need to have know-how when you start playing a Bigger Game. You just need to have a hunger mighty enough to fuel your will – and then the work itself will pull you forward.

Dialing it up

The lucky ones among us already know the impact they want to have in their communities, their companies, and their world. The rest of us need to get hungry and stay hungry if we want to play a Bigger Game.

Here's how to start dialing up your wanter: get conscious. Keep your eyes and ears open. Look and feel around you for what has heart and meaning. Notice what leaves you flat and what has resonance for you – that deep, physical vibration of attunement that lets you know you're in the territory of fulfillment.

Then, practice wanting whatever you want. Maybe this includes a really hefty diamond ring, a Porsche 914, or a major promotion. Cool. The important thing at first is simply to be conscious of yourself as the "wanter" and to wake up your hunger. So bring it on. Make a list. The more wants, the better.

Seek into the field

As you keep paying attention to what's going on inside you – both the hunger pangs and the resonance – begin looking outside yourself for clues and triggers to the wants of your soul. Read avidly. Talk to your friends, colleagues, and neighbors about what they see and what is needed. Learn all you can about what's going on in your world. When questions of "Who me?" or "How?" or "Can I?" rise in you, let them go and just keep going. "How" doesn't matter yet and will only stall or thwart your exploration. Hunger matters hugely.

Explore the fields that touch your life. What do you want for these fields? What do you want for your company? Your work team? The people who live on your block? What do you want for the students, the teachers, the administrators, and/or the parents of your son's school? For your neighborhood? For the employees of your company and/or the company itself? For corporate America? For the nonprofit organization whose board you serve? For your industry or profession? For the arts? For the environmental or sustainability movements? For ending world hunger? For growing peace? For urban sprawl? For women on welfare? For equal rights? For animals?

And sometimes, when we're paying attention, we'll see somebody else's Bigger Game, fall in love with it, and hunger to make it our own. Originality is not important here. In fact, there is probably no Bigger Game under the sun that is entirely new. What matters is waking up the hunger for meaning, the yearning to contribute and leave our thumbprint on some piece of our world.

No, not that! Something is missing. Yes, more of that!
As you look for ways to increase the volume of your "wanter," you might want to explore your world through the following three lenses:

1) No, not that!
Sometimes our hunger is aroused by tragedy, loss, or outrage in the field. Drunk drivers killing children. Discrimination against people of color. World terrorism. Women dying of breast cancer. No, not that! This must never happen again! Our hunger becomes a wake-up call to action.

2) Something is missing.
Sometimes we look into the field and it becomes clear that something is missing. Neighbors don't have a place to congregate. Cancer research results are not consolidated and widely available. There is plenty of food and plenty of hungry people, and the former isn't reaching the latter. Teachers are not getting the recognition and remuneration they need to stay motivated and to attract

the very best to the profession. Our hunger to provide what's missing becomes the wake-up call to action.

3) Yes, more of that!
Sometimes we glimpse something wonderful and crave more of that. A vision for cooperative community development based on principles of sustainability. One summer evening concert in the park that could blossom into a nightly event. A public transportation system that really works. Our hunger to create more of what's already working becomes our wake-up call to action.

Focus these lenses within yourself and outside yourself simultaneously. What do you want? What does the field want? Where do your personal hunger and the hunger in the field intersect? Remember, when your hunger marries the hunger in the field, a compelling purpose is born.

Staying hungry
This book is not about *having* a Bigger Game. It is about being a Bigger Game player who knows how to get hungry, connect with purpose, find a game, make a difference, own the growth, and hunger for the next level of play. A Bigger Game player is always somewhere on the Bigger Game Board, and hunger – the very antithesis of complacency – is a totally valid place to be playing. So as you wake up your hunger to make a difference, please resist the following temptations to go back to sleep:

• Do not ask "how?" when you're hungering. When that word volunteers itself, say "no thanks" for now. There's plenty of time for "how?" after you've committed to the compelling purpose of "I will." And remember, ordinary people rise to do extraordinary things all the time.

• Do not compare yourself to others' hunger, goals, or accomplishments. What you want and the need you see in the field is exactly the Bigger Game for you. And yes, you are big enough to be a player.

• Do not listen to yourself or other people say "you can't." You actually don't know whether you can or not; so as long as you're making it up anyway, you might as well make up the belief that "you can."

• Do not allow the discomfort of ambiguity or "I don't know" send you back into a comfort zone. Developing a strong tolerance for not knowing is a key skill for all Bigger Game players.

• Do not put a stopwatch on how long you "should" hunger before finding the Bigger Game that lights your fire. Some people dwell in the hunger zone for a year or more until their Bigger Game finds them. And it's a great idea to keep at least one foot here all the time in order to make your game bigger and make sure it's still the right one for you.

So, let your stomach growl and your heart yearn – and yearn and yearn and yearn some more. Remember Mother Theresa. If you can learn to welcome the hunger pangs of the soul, you are stepping up to be a player.

Summary

- Once our physical survival is assured, all human beings hunger for a meaningful life in which they use their gifts to contribute to what they care about.

- Hunger – the search for what has purpose, meaning, and resonance – is an integral component of finding and playing a Bigger Game.

- It is uncomfortable to hunger for what we don't have, especially when we don't know how to get it. It is equally uncomfortable not to know what it is we hunger for. Because our culture promotes quick fixes, we have learned many ways to distract and numb ourselves so we don't have to think about the difference we yearn to make. The truth is that we will never find a Bigger Game if we're not willing to "dial up our wanters" and endure the hunger pangs that follow.

- To get in touch with what we deeply want, it's important to stay conscious, listen, read, and seek into the field without getting stalled by the demands of "how" or the ambiguity of the unknown.

- It's important for us to pay attention to two sources of hunger – within ourselves and within the field around us. The intersection between what we want for ourselves and what is wanted out there in the field is the birthplace of compelling purpose.

- The hunger that leads to a Bigger Game tends to arise from three sources:

  1) No, not that!
  2) Something is missing.
  3) Yes, more of that!

Chapter 7
Compelling Purpose and Naming the Game

In the last chapter, you asked the question "What do I hunger for?" And you experimented with different ways to dial up your "wanter" and create raw material from your hunger. Now your job is to identify what part of your hunger is most compelling – what pulls at you the most. The answer to that question is your compelling purpose. A compelling purpose is your best expression of who you are and what you care about. This chapter focuses on helping you to articulate the kind of purpose that provides a good enough reason to play a Bigger Game – and the process of naming the game itself.

First, a word or two about purpose. Many thoughtful people have spent considerable time thinking about their personal life purpose. This work zeroes in on your current and desired state of being through such questions as: Who am I? Who do I want to become? What are my inherent gifts? What competencies and qualities of character do I wish to cultivate? What activities and accomplishments will enable me to use and develop my natural gifts? What was I born on this earth to create? What do I want my life to have been about?

A personal purpose is, in essence, what you're here for and how you want to be used by life. Exploring your life purpose is hugely worthwhile and is a useful reference point when you're playing a Bigger Game. After all, "designing who you are becoming" is an underlying concept of the Bigger Game, and your vision of who you aspire to become is certainly part of what fuels your hunger.

An exploration of life purpose starts from the inside out, requiring deep self-reflection. Compelling purpose, at least as we define it here, arises as a response to what calls you and pulls at you from outside in your world. The purpose that gives rise to Bigger Games is born of raw hunger – yours plus the hunger "out there" in the field. When the two intersect, the result is resonance and a new entity that is both unique and greater than the sum of its parts.

Of course, you'll want to find a compelling purpose and a Bigger Game that make the best use of you – your singular talents, aptitudes, and abilities. However, "best use of me" is not the be-all and end-all for choosing your game. Find what you care about most – what has the strongest pull on you. And then, when you have defined your purpose and your game, find where you are best used within it, and recruit allies to do the rest.

A Bigger Game calls you and pulls at you. It never pushes or forces. If you are feeling push, force, or "have to," this probably isn't your compelling purpose.

What is the process that gets you from where you are to a clear sense of compelling purpose? The questions to be asking yourself include: What am I about? What must happen in my corner of the world? What is needed in my company, community, industry, neighborhood, state, or country? What do I absolutely deplore? What most invigorates and inspires me? What must stop? What is no longer acceptable? What do I yearn to create that is truly needed out there? To find the answers, seek out what is needed – and then notice your own response to what you discover. How much resonance resides in you as you look out? Notice what pulls and calls to you.

There is a paradox at work here: The game is not about you or your team; it is about the field. And yet, it is all about you because it touches your soul deeply.

From many to one: MOST compelling purpose

When your eyes and ears and heart are open and you give your soul's hunger license to speak, you will likely be moved by many purposes that respond to needs out there. After all, you have a complex, multifaceted life, and there are many things that are important to you. It's not unusual, in fact, for people to have ten or 20 purposes that exert a considerable tug on them. That's great. The more, the better. As a Bigger Game player, though, what you want to find is that one purpose that pulls at you the most – the one that has the most resonance for you right now. It is this compelling purpose that becomes the platform for naming your Bigger Game.

By the way, your compelling purpose and your Bigger Game are deeply intertwined, yet they are not one and the same. Your compelling purpose is a vision of what must happen in your world; it should be too ambitious to ever be accomplished in full. Your Bigger Game, on the other hand, is one specific vehicle for bringing your compelling purpose to life. A Bigger Game is something tangible that can be accomplished and completed, only to be replaced by the next vehicle for manifesting your compelling purpose.

Here's an example. One compelling purpose might be: "Conserve precious resources." A Bigger Game to support this purpose might be: "By the end of the year, get every supermarket in my community to sell reusable cloth bags and give customers a discount for using cloth instead of paper or plastic." Once this Bigger Game is accomplished, it becomes a new game that ups the ante, such as "Take the cloth grocery bag campaign countywide... then statewide... then national... then global!" And so it goes.

We'll be returning to these distinctions later in this chapter. First, though, let's look at the process of pinning down the purposes that have the most pull for you. You've already spent some time exploring your hunger in the last chapter. Now you can use what you've learned as the basis to deepen your exploration of purpose.

Before you narrow your search to the one purpose that compels you the most, we'll give you a bunch of different ways to open up your exploration and check out lots of possibilities.

Imagine...

Quiet your mind and get in touch with the hunger you've felt before. What do you want? It may be something related to your home life, your work life, your community, or your hobbies. Next, look at world events, economic circumstances in this country and elsewhere, the health of your neighborhood, the conditions of your workplace. Notice if you have a sense of how you'd like it to be different. A different way of working, a new way of creating, relating, or innovating. If "how" and "reality" were not issues, what is it that you'd want?

Explore a feeling you have at work or elsewhere – something you want for others. Sense it in your body. Or locate a realm that's important to you and notice what change you want within this field. It yearns for something to be more, to be less, to be new. What is that?

Notice where your attention is called. For example, do you want to improve morale in your workplace? Create more dignified living conditions for impoverished elders? Provide resources for stretched-thin entrepreneurs? Expand storytelling hours at the public library? Extend the jogging path network throughout your town's park system? Create an awards program to provide recognition to children with special needs and gifts? Find an area where you want to focus your attention and allow yourself to want something that's big and daring and different for it.

Notice the thoughts of "How" and "Who, me?" that creep into your mind now and then – and banish them. There will be plenty of time to figure all that out later.

What is it that you burn to create? What must happen? Dare to know without having to know how. What calls you most deeply?

What has the most resonance?

In order to focus your exploration, try completing the following statements:

- What I want for my family is...
- What I want for people at my organization is...
- My job would be better if...
- Humankind would be better off if...
- What I want for my children/the next generation is...
- People are at their best when...
- I could do better on the job if...
- In the workplace, my soul hungers for...
- If "how" were no object, what I'd really want is...
- What hurts me to think about is...

The three lenses for finding compelling purpose
Now let's focus the purpose discovery process a bit more narrowly. In the last chapter, we touched on how Bigger Games generally arise from three basic sources, three sets of lenses through which we see the world. Take an opportunity to revisit these lenses now, using what you know about your soul's hunger to move toward a compelling purpose that pulls you along like a ski lift on a snowy day.

1) No, not that!
The first lens is "No, not that!" Perhaps you remember the old movie *Network*, in which a deranged anchorman persuaded millions of viewers to stick their heads out the window and bellow, "I'm mad as hell and I'm not going to take it anymore!" That's what "No, not that" is about. It represents an outraged refusal to put up with what is intolerable for one more minute.

"No, not that!" is what inspired union worker Norma Rae to lead a strike to improve intolerable working conditions. "No, not that!" inspired Patty Wetterling, whose son Jacob was abducted, to help put missing children on milk cartons. "No, not that!" inspired Alice Coles' stand to keep a prison out of her community. "No, not that!" was the impetus that led to the formation of Mothers Against Drunk Driving (MADD), the Green Peace initiative to stop the bludgeoning of baby seals, and Nelson Mandela to fight the apartheid that had ripped his beloved country in two.

Answering the questions below may help you articulate the "No, not that!" hunger that lives in you:

- What are two things in your world that just don't work?
- What injustices outrage you?
- What must not happen?
- What pain exists that is just not OK with you?
- What are your recurring complaints about your world or the people in it?

2) Something is missing.

Yet another major source of Bigger Games is "What's missing?" What do I want and need that doesn't exist yet – that the field wants, too? Examples of Bigger Games born from this spring include: Entrepreneur Ted Turner's decision to create an all-news cable television network he called CNN. The Sundance Institute and its accompanying film festival, founded by Robert Redford to provide support and recognition for emerging independent filmmakers. The Doyle Street Co-Housing Project in Emeryville, California, designed nearly 20 years ago by architects and life partners Katherine McCammack and Charles Durrett as America's pioneering venture into the co-housing intentional community movement.

Here are some questions that may stimulate your hunger for what you yearn to create from scratch:

- What needs to start?
- What is the ultimate freedom you can envision for human beings?
- What's a service or program you wish existed for your children? For you?
- What must happen for the sake of future generations?
- What are your recurring complaints about your world?
- What do you want to prevent other people from experiencing?

- For what do you search the Yellow Pages... in vain?
- What innovations are being made in other countries that aren't in this country yet?
- If you had a magic wand, what would you create?

3) Yes, more of that!

Another source of Bigger Games is "Yes, more of that!" What is already working that you – and the field – want to increase? Here are some examples: Isolated corporate quality initiatives that coalesced into a companywide campaign to earn the Malcolm Baldridge Award. An inspiring book on emotional intelligence that segued into emotional intelligence training programs in organizations worldwide. Peter Newport's campaign to increase interest and participation in his beloved sport, sailplaning. Support groups for parents of cancer victims that emerged out of caring conversations. Neighborhood potluck suppers that evolved into the international co-housing movement toward intentional community. Habitat for Humanity, which started as a local initiative and rapidly spread around the United States. All of these are examples of Bigger Games that represent the augmentation of what's already working.

You may want to use the questions below to help you articulate what you want more of:

- What is most inspiring and uplifting about people?
- What's one thing you love about your neighborhood that you'd like to see expand citywide?
- What works in your company or other companies to build respect and collegiality?
- What would it be like if these qualities were descriptors for corporate America?
- What volunteer programs in your community do you find most inspiring?

Naming your game

The game you choose is but one vehicle for moving your compelling purpose forward. Your game may change while your purpose remains as constant as the North Star.

You'll want the name of your game to be specific, measurable, easy to remember, and inspiring – to you, anyway. It doesn't matter if the name of your game inspires anybody else. That's what a compelling purpose is for.

Here are some examples of Bigger Game names:

• Transform the culture in my organization to one characterized by "hungry learners."
• Bring co-active coaching into prisons.
• Build and rebuild homes in rural Kentucky.
• Document residents of my block with a photograph album.
• Create a neighborhood watch program.
• Bring people to Bali to study happiness.

Notice that these names are pretty simple, and that they meet the following criteria:

• Is a measurement element built into the game? Can you tell from the name whether or not you'll know when you have accomplished it?
• Is there an action verb that gives you something specific and inspiring to do?
• Is the name less than eight words (so that it's really easy to remember and speak out loud)?
• Does the game have the potential to evolve into a new iteration within 3-12 months? (If not, it may be too big for now and you'll need to define the "game before the game.")
• Does the name give you something of a roadmap for what you'll be doing each day?
• Does the name of your game make you vibrate? Make you gulp?
• In each moment, does the name tell you if you are on track or not?
• Does the game serve a specific population and drive toward a specific result?

And lest this assignment seem so weighty that you want to go back to bed and pull the covers over your head, know that what's most important is simply to get something down on paper. Dare to pick a game. Any game. It doesn't have to be the "right" game. The words don't have to be right. The concept doesn't have to be right. Nothing has to be right. Do it in pencil with a nice fat eraser on the end. Just get something down so that you have a name to react to, to play with, to modify, to adapt. Let yourself name a different game every day for a week or a month. Just get started until you find a game and a name for it that make your knees buckle with sheer excitement.

Grappling with the gulp
You've captured your notes on hunger, comfort zones, and your most compelling purpose of all (for now, at least). You have identified the Bigger Game you want to play and given it a moniker. If your game is truly a worthy challenge for you, the "gulp" should have you by the throat just about now. Actually, you've probably been feeling some sense of "Who do I think I am to take this on?" throughout the discovery process. The gulp is a good thing. It means you're right on track. In the next chapter, we'll talk about how to use the tremendous energy of the gulp to keep you centered on the playing field of your Bigger Game.

Summary

• Your personal life purpose is a useful reference point for who you wish to become... and it's all about you. The compelling purpose, which gives rise to Bigger Games, focuses on what's wanted in the field, too.

• A compelling purpose is born out of raw, pulsating hunger – the hunger out there and the hunger within you. When the two collide, the result is resonance and a new entity that is both unique and greater than the sum of its parts.

• A compelling purpose has a "pull" energy; it is a good enough reason to choose the path that is less safe and comfortable – for the sake of your game.

• A compelling purpose and the name of the game are different. A compelling purpose is a vision of what must happen in your world; it should be too ambitious to ever be accomplished in full. Your Bigger Game, on the other hand, is one specific vehicle for bringing your compelling purpose to life.

• The three basic sources of Bigger Games in the world are "No, Not That!" "Something is Missing," and "Yes, More of That!" In finding your own game, it's useful to identify the major realms of your life and look at each through these three lenses.

A sampling of Game Names

Here are some examples of Bigger Game names developed by the players who have come through our workshops:

- Create 20 Encouragement Centers for Israeli and Palestinian children ages 10-15 by 2010.

- Deliver a sustainable anti-trafficking program for victims of modern day slavery in South Florida by March 2006.

- Make San Diego the most desirable place for seniors to live.

- Create and produce a TV series called *Global Charity* by September 2006.

- Raise $1 million for an outdoor retreat center for teens.

- Implement a "Living the Values" program at our company.

- Create and implement an environment that makes our employees the #1 priority.

- Improve customer perception of the pharmaceutical industry's role in society.

- Create "One Business Banking Team."

- Transform human interaction in the advertising industry.

- Create an incubator for a new style of leadership within our company.

Chapter 8
The Gulp

The Gulp:

- Is the feeling of scary exhilaration when you know you must do something yet have no idea how you will do it.
- Occurs when your existing competencies are not sufficient for you to succeed at your Bigger Game.
- Is walking into ambiguity, taking step after step on an unmarked path.
- Is accompanied by sweaty palms as you realize you will be exposed to the risk of failing.
- Is present... or you may not be playing a Bigger Game.

The gulp is the point in the Bigger Game where "I must" and "I can't" intersect. In this chapter, we'll be looking at the anatomy of the gulp, and how to use it to your advantage in playing your Bigger Game.

As you've moved through the process of exploring your hunger and identifying your compelling purpose, you have doubtless experienced many "gulp moments." They occur when you hear an inner voice saying, "I don't have time" or "This is too big for me" or "I've got to make a living" or "Who do I think I am?" or "It will be too difficult." Some of these voices represent comfort zones – habitual, knee-jerk ways of thinking and behaving.

As you contemplate your compelling purpose, those voices keep hammering inside your brain: "I don't know how to make this happen." "Wait and see." "I don't know enough yet." "I've got to make a comprehensive plan." This is part of a common comfort zone in our culture that tells us not to move until all the pieces are in place, all the steps are planned out, and all contingencies accounted for. This comfort zone is one that causes many people to turn back, walking away from their calling for fear of the unknown.

That's in general. How about you personally? Maybe you've got some glimmers around your compelling purpose, maybe even spotted your Bigger Game, and you care fiercely about making it happen. You really do. And it's time for the rubber to start connecting with the road. You've had quite a few "gulpy" moments along the way, of course, but at this point, you are approaching the doorway to a big-time gulp. The one where people tend to get sweaty palms and dry mouths and feel their hearts beating faster and louder.

The gulp is a necessary and predictable sign that you are on the right track and that your Bigger Game is big enough for you. Why? The person you are at this moment cannot achieve your Bigger Game. It demands more capabilities from you than you currently have in your bag of tricks. You need to grow new skills, competencies, and qualities of character – and there are no guarantees of success. That's enough to intimidate most anybody at least a little. So if you're not gulping, you're probably not gaining new competencies. If you're not gulping, most likely your game has gone flat or a little bit small. If you're not gulping, your game may not be big enough to grow you. Uncomfortable though it may be, then, the gulp is good for Bigger Game players – good for your personal evolution and good for the purpose you're working to bring to life.

Remember the four-step model of embodied learning we offered back in Chapter 5? The first step was Unconscious Incompetence, or "you don't know that you don't know – and ignorance is bliss." The second step of the model – Conscious Incompetence – is the territory of the gulp. You know what you don't know, and there's a yawning gap between what you've got and what you want. As much as we'd all like to bypass this stage of learning, it is as inevitable as it is uncomfortable. And the prospect of Conscious Incompetence dead ahead is a big part of what makes us gulp.

Gulp distinctions
Now, there are several kinds of gulps that Bigger Game players experience. Some of them are useful and some are not.

1) Gulpus Interruptus
First, let's look at what we'll call "gulpus interruptus." This happens when the comfort zone of self-sabotaging thinking kicks in to "save" you before you've even experienced any real fear or the sensations associated with it. "This is gonna be too hard for me, so I'll stop thinking about it and clear out e-mails instead." The gulp is nipped in the bud – and so is your Bigger Game.

2) Overwhelm Gulp
Next comes the "overwhelm gulp." "I'm too busy." "I don't know how." "I don't know where to start." "I've never done it before so what makes me think I can do this now?" The predominant theme here is "I can't." If this form of gulp gets you by the throat, it can be paralyzing, drain all the energy out of you, and shut you down so that you want nothing more than to crawl into bed and pull the quilt over your head. If the thought of your Bigger Game inspires panic, horror, and dread in you, this may be a sign that the game you've chosen is too big. In that case, you may need to seek out the game before this game – or another one altogether – something that's a good hefty stretch for you, but not totally horrifying. Remember, if your game doesn't have the power to pull you past the gulp, it may not really be your game.

3) Essential Gulp

Finally, we have the "essential gulp." Whereas the overwhelm gulp was enervating, this gulp is as energizing and exhilarating as a steep climb up a hill on a roller coaster. "I may not know how, but... this must be and it's up to me." Wheee! This gulp represents the intersection between "I must" and "I can't." It is the gulp that calls you forth to stand tall, take a deep breath, and swing into bold action.

Before we leave these distinctions, it's useful to talk about what grows the gulp and what shrinks it to manageable proportions.

Growing and shrinking the gulp

If you didn't have a brain filled with life experience, no situation or challenge in the world would have the power to faze you. (You'd probably be in trouble because your brain didn't remind you to look both ways before crossing the street, but that's another matter.) The fact is, however, you do have a brain, and it's chock-full of automatic danger signals based on your personal history and experience.

As we alluded to when discussing comfort zones, all the mental and sensory input that comes your way goes first to and through your amygdala. That's the primitive, reptilian part of your brain that's located at the base of your skull. Your amygdala grunts out instructions to fight, freeze, or flee at any sign of danger. The amygdala knows what's dangerous based on your history of what's caused trouble in the past. It's quite the alarmist, the amygdala is. It doesn't stop to consider whether something really does pose a threat; it routinely sets off sirens at any hint of trouble. "Better safe than sorry" is its modus operandi.

After your reptile brain has done its job, the rest of your brain kicks in to analyze whether danger actually exists or if the amygdala was just blowing smoke again. Your thinking brain may indeed say "false alarm, nothing to fear here." It is just as likely, however, to build a righteous case for fear by referring back to all the incidents in your personal history where you were hurt or embarrassed.

How does this work vis-à-vis the gulp? Well, let's say you have just named an ambitious Bigger Game and it's scaring the daylights out of you. Your forehead is sweating, your stomach is lurching, and you can't drink enough water to moisten your dry mouth. You can't help but notice this gulp – it's like neon signs at midnight in Las Vegas.

You are at an important choice point here. If you let your brain run rampant, it will refer back to your history and project ahead to your future to give you lots of good reasons to be afraid, *be very afraid*. This, of course, only has the effect of heightening the gulp until it has the potential to overwhelm and paralyze you. On the other hand, if you concentrate on staying present and moving into action, you need only contend with the gulp at hand rather than the mega-gulp produced by your own imaginings.

Let's try an example. You are scaling the sheer face of a mountainside. You are pretty high up and tired, and you can't find a foothold for your next move. Your amygdala shouts, "Watch out, you're gonna fall and *die*!" If you let your thinking brain jump on this bandwagon, it will likely recall all the climbers who have perished under similar circumstances plus all the other awful things that could happen in a tumble from this altitude. This kind of thinking does not energize you or help you to find your next foothold.

Try this instead. You are pretty high up and tired, and you can't find a foothold for your next move. You take a deep breath and notice what's going on in your body. Oh my, there's some fear here, and in addition to my dry mouth, a lot of new energy is available in this gulp! You are wide-awake, fully present, and alert. You look up and see plenty of handholds and footholds not too far above you. You look down to see footholds below you in case you need to turn back. You remember that your rope is right here, supporting you. You stabilize yourself with most of your weight on your hands and move into action, feeling the wall with your foot for a crevice that will support your weight. Oh, there it is! And you move boldly.

The gulp is real and it's important for you to pay attention to it. At the same time, you have the choice to feed it or to let it be as it is and use its energy to move through the gulp into action. If you want to play a Bigger Game, you're going to find that the latter approach works much, much more efficiently for you.

In fact, the process of staying present through the gulp without overthinking is at the heart of what Mihaly Csikszentmihalyi characterizes as the experience of "flow." As he says in his book *Flow: The Psychology of Optimal Experience*: "When all a person's relevant skills are needed to cope with the challenges of a situation, that person's attention is completely absorbed by the activity. There is no excess psychic energy left over to process any information but what the activity offers. All the attention is concentrated on the relevant stimuli. As a result, one of the most universal and distinctive features of optimal experience takes place: People become so involved in what they are doing that the activity becomes spontaneous, almost automatic; they stop being aware of themselves as separate from the actions they are performing." Again, when you move into action, the gulp tends to disappear as you become one with your Bigger Game.

A good enough reason

When your soul's hunger is not being fed or your purpose is not compelling enough or your Bigger Game is not important enough, comfort zones will carry the day every time and your game will never get past the idea stage. This is neither good nor bad; it's just the way human beings operate. We need a good enough reason to endure the discomfort of challenging the status quo.

Now, there are lots of reasons that are good enough to inspire us to try something new. Wanting to look good in a swimsuit can be a good enough reason to eat less and exercise more. Wanting to see your kids graduate from college can be a good enough reason to stop destroying your liver with that old devil, rum. Craving the thrill of an adrenaline rush may be a good enough reason to fling yourself off a bridge with a rubber band tied to your feet. So we're not claiming that compelling purpose fueled by raging soul hunger is the only good enough reason to step through the gulp into action.... In our experience, though, compelling purpose is hard to beat as a good enough reason.

What sets Bigger Game players apart is their willingness to

embrace the gulp for the sake of their compelling purpose, and jump into bold action with both feet, like Butch Cassidy and the Sundance kid leaping over the cliff without regard to their swimming abilities – or lack thereof. Bigger Game players invite the gulp for the sake of manifesting their compelling purpose, doing what they must do in the world, and living a life rich with heart and meaning. Bring it on. Here I come.

Experiencing the gulp

Because the gulp is so valuable, we're asking you to notice it – even welcome it – then feel it and step right through it into action, fueled by a compelling purpose and, more often than not, a little help from your friends. Learning how to experience the gulp and step through it is, in fact, one of the most important catalysts to your personal development you'll ever have. If the games you play design who you are becoming, the ability to step through the gulp, time and time again, is what ensures that you will become all that you can be.

Mastering domains vs. mastering process

You feel the gulp, take a deep breath, put your attention "over there," and move into new territory. After doing the new thing that scares you a time or two, it's no longer a stretch and even begins to evolve into a new, albeit advanced comfort zone because what once was bold is now effortless. And now you're ready to take on the next challenge in the next domain.

So here you are, stepping through gulps and routinely ticking the domains you've conquered off your list. Public speaking – made two speeches, more scheduled. Check. Not a big deal anymore. Six-figure fund-raising requests – four of them, complete with PowerPoint presentations. Check. Piece of cake. Enrolling area CEOs in my new Executive Council. Check. Easy. Jumping out of an airplane. Did that yesterday. Check. Done.

You see, there is not one Big Gulp, but rather lots of gulpworthy challenges for you to explore. Gulp work is like a dance: gulp/step/fail/learn, gulp/step/soar/learn, gulp/step/fail/learn, gulp/step/succeed/learn....

And before you've been doing the dance for all that long, you'll find that you not only have mastered a variety of domains – specific areas of activities that don't have the power to scare you anymore – you've also mastered the process of stepping through gulps into bold action across all domains.

In other words, the more seasoned you become at moving in the face of fear, the more faith you have in yourself to make it through to the other side just fine, no matter what the challenge may be. As a result, you shorten the gap between gulp and action, and your recovery time is accelerated as well. This is a boon, because most of the fear associated with the gulp exists only in the gap between thinking something up and going for it. As you master the process, it gets easier to assess your failings dispassionately for the learning rather than attach yourself to your hideous blunders. You become tough and bouncy, resilient and resourceful. Your attention is consistently on the field and you are performing at a high level across the boards, moving and shaking. You know from experience that failing is no big deal and, because tragedy plus time equals comedy, you have lots of amusing war stories to relate. Your power and impact are growing off the charts. You're playing a game that has you becoming the person you really want to be.

The author and filmmaker Michael Moore is a great example of mastering the gulp process to move into increasingly high levels of performance. Moore began his career in Detroit as a social activist and journalist. A self-described "shy person" and introvert, he had to steel himself before every interview. Before too long, Moore figured that making a movie would be a high-impact way to get airtime for his views. For the sake of his Bigger Game, he mastered the art of confrontation. In order to make his films *Bowling for Columbine* (a lively examination of America's deadly gun culture), and *Fahrenheit 911* (a scathing denunciation of the Bush administration), he stepped through gulp after gulp as he inserted himself into situations with high embarrassment potential. As a result of all this experience, Moore has achieved considerable mastery of the gulp/move/learn process. It takes a lot to scare him these days. And he probably has as many amusing war stories to relate as there are stars in the sky.

Enjoying the gulp
The gulp is a big part of why playing a Bigger Game is the biggest fun you can possibly have. After all, what could be more satisfying than moving toward something that scares you and emerging triumphant on the other side? As a result, some people not only stop minding the discomfort of the gulp; they come to enjoy gulp experiences in their lives... a lot. That's the appeal for participants in thrill sports like hang gliding, rock climbing, or ski jumping.

It is our fervent hope that you develop a capacity and even an appetite for the gulp. You'll need it to play a Bigger Game. And it is important that you be able to distinguish the line between real and perceived danger. Most of what scares us around our Bigger Games is not actually life-threatening. More often than not, the worst that can happen is that we will fail to achieve our intended outcome and/or embarrass ourselves. No big deal. Sometimes, though, a gulp may foretell a genuine danger. Just as you don't want to be jumping off a cliff without a parachute, you don't want to be quitting your day job for the sake of your Bigger Game if you don't know how you're going to feed your family. That brings us back around to assessment, the cool-headed partner of bold action. When you are seeing things clearly, you can trust your game to dictate your next move. When you live on the Bigger Game Board – using it as a way to orient your life – you'll know what to do.

It's All Made Up
Rick Tamlyn chose "It's All Made Up" as the name for his training business because human beings go a long way toward creating the lives they want through the power of their thoughts and beliefs. After all, any thought we have about the future is mere projection. Even though our past experience may give us a plausible scenario for what's likely to happen next, we can never be sure what will actually come to pass. So we make up what's going to happen without any way of knowing the truth. And we create mental constructs for what we view as right or wrong, good or bad, up or down. We construct in living color what we see as our world and our future... and we then tend to invent self-fulfilling prophecies that impede our growth and mire us in what's most safe, predict-

able, and boring.

The Bigger Game is an opportunity to intentionally create a life and a contribution that truly compels and fulfills us. It is a way to create a self-fulfilling prophecy about what we want our lives to stand for and be. As a part of this process, we have the opportunity to make up the belief that gulping with fear is the coolest activity since cavemen rubbed two sticks together to create fire because of its power in designing who we are becoming.

So, as long as you're making your life up anyway, why not make up that it's way cool to surmount fear, and then step into the dance of the gulp with unmitigated enthusiasm. What doesn't kill you makes you stronger, it's true. And you might just find that stepping through the gulp – and then doing it again – not only doesn't kill you... but it becomes a source of vast pleasure and satisfaction.

Summary

• The gulp is the point in the Bigger Game where "I must" and "I can't" intersect.

• The gulp is a necessary and predictable indicator that your Bigger Game is big enough to grow you. Uncomfortable though it may be, the gulp means you're on the right track.

• There are three kinds of gulp:

  - Gulpus Interruptus occurs when the comfort zone of self-sabotaging thinking nips the gulp – and your game – in the bud. "This is too hard; I'll return e-mails instead."
  - The Overwhelm Gulp focuses on "I can't" to the point where you shut down. This may signal that the game you've chosen is too big.
  - Finally, the Essential Gulp is as energizing and exhilarating as a steep climb up to the top of a roller coaster. "I may not know how, but... this must be and it's up to me." Wheee! It is the gulp that calls you forth into bold action.

• Staying fully present in assessing what's happening is a great way to notice the gulp and capitalize on its energy.

• After moving through the gulp into action in a number of domains, you begin to master the process of gulp management. This is perhaps your most valuable catalyst to personal growth.

• Some people become gulp aficionados and deliberately seek its energy. Assessment will help you distinguish between the thrill you crave and what your game is wanting from you.

Section Three
How Do I Play My Bigger Game?

By 1992, Microsoft founder Bill Gates had given away more than $21 million to Seattle-area charities and schools – a tidy sum, yes, yet miserly given his immense wealth. Totally immersed in his company, Gates planned to wait 20-30 years until retiring to focus on giving, but the challenge of "stupid poverty" – people dying for want of a $2 pill because they live on $1 a day – accelerated that schedule. In addition to investing many billions of dollars, Gates and his wife, Melinda, are investing their own time, compassion, and second-to-none business acumen to forge the alliances and pinpoint the grantees that can improve the most lives most efficiently. Bill and Melinda Gates have arrived at a compelling purpose that is nothing less than Ending Poverty on This Planet, and their Bigger Game has morphed into the largest, highest-impact foundation in the world.

While Bill and Melinda Gates are wealthy beyond measure, Alice Coles was among the poorest of the poor. Coles and her neighbors used to live in dilapidated shacks without running water in rural Bayview, Virginia. Nothing had changed there in several generations, until plans to build a huge, maximum-security prison in the community became the last straw for Coles. Her "No, not that!" forestalled the prison project while giving her a glimpse of what one outraged woman can do when she sets her mind to it. Building on her success at blocking the prison project, her Bigger Game morphed to focus on "What's missing?" Thanks to her widespread alliances and investment in fund-raising training and public speaking, Coles became the catalyst in transforming her worst-of-the-worst neighborhood into a national model for what can happen when people take a stand for decent homes, hot running water, and human dignity.

Anything is possible when you jump in and start playing your Bigger Game.

You've been on the Bigger Game Board ever since you chose to be a player. You're much more conscious than you used to be – conscious of your comfort zones and their costs and benefits, conscious of what you want and what you don't want, conscious of your soul's hunger for richness and meaning, conscious of where you are on the Game Board, assessing the impact of your last bold action, adjusting your course accordingly, and reading the field to tell you where to go next. You are aware of your own competencies and character and how you intend to develop yourself. You are awake. You are a player.

You've learned to listen to the hunger of your soul and the hunger in the various areas of your life. You've explored compelling purposes and found the one that has the most pull for you, for now. You've defined a Bigger Game – a vehicle for advancing your purpose – that thrills you. And you're ready and eager to play, despite or maybe because of the gulp that rises in your throat every time you think about your game and who you'll have to become to see it through.

And now it's time for the rubber to meet the road in a new way. It's time to make your Bigger Game real. The final chapters of this book focus on the process of manifesting your Bigger Game – and preparing for the next one.

You can't assess how you're doing if you don't have metrics to measure against. A Bigger Game requires a game plan that lays out the key results you want to achieve – and by when. You need to have your outcomes in place so you know what you're shooting for. Along the way, of course, circumstances will change and so will you, which means you'll need to assess and reassess your game plan constantly. You can always reconfigure your targets, but you have to have targets in order to reconfigure them. So if you were thinking of your plan as a pristine document that rests in honor on your top bookshelf, think again. We're talking coffee stains and scribbles, erasures, and lots of blank paper.

Your game plan must include the elements of investments, allies, and sustainability. What investments do you need to make in yourself as a Bigger Game player? Are you healthy and energetic? If not, how do you need to alter your diet and exercise habits? Do you have sufficient time to play your game? If not, what resources do you need to free you up, organize you, and make you more efficient? What education and competencies do you need right up front? Do you need accreditation in a particular field? Practice in public speaking? Computer literacy training? Fund-raising acumen?

Developing strategic alliances is a key element of investing in yourself and your Bigger Game. Allies include your constituents, cheerleaders, sounding boards, co-players, expert resources, the media... even those naysayers who serve to stiffen your resolve. Remember, a Bigger Game is by the people and for the people. If you can play it all by yourself, it may not be a Bigger Game.

Once you have invested in yourself and forged alliances to build a powerful infrastructure for getting your Bigger Game going, how will you keep it going? How do you ensure that you will continue to be up to the demands of your game? And how do you ensure that your game itself has sufficient momentum and resources to go on without you if you're ready to go on to something else? After all, if everything falls apart the moment you disappear, your Bigger Game is really a self-game, isn't it? So we'll be looking at what creates sustainability in these chapters, too.

And finally, metamorphosis – or evolution to the next incarnation – is embedded in the very nature of a Bigger Game. You reach your goal and it's time to find another one. Or you near your goal and changes in the field dictate a retooled outcome. You gain more competence and confidence and your Bigger Game just doesn't seem ambitious enough anymore. Your co-players offer new skills, ideas, and contacts to grow the dream. A door slams shut while the outline of another door reveals itself in what seemed to be a seamless wall. It is impossible to predict in advance what will happen, and how your Bigger Game will evolve. It's like standing on the side of a curvy river trying to predict each eddy and rapid that lies ahead. Once you get in your boat, dip your oar into the water, and begin to move forward, new obstacles and opportunities will be revealed along the way, and your game will morph. We'll be talking about that, too.

You have defined your Bigger Game. And even if you haven't, you now know that you are always somewhere on the Game Board. You're in the boat. The river is shining before you and you can just barely hear a few rapids in the distance... gulp.

Ready to move? Dip those oars.

Chapter 9
Your Game Plan

You and/or your team have settled on the compelling purpose that stirs your soul and feeds your hunger. You may or may not have named a Bigger Game – a measurable way to move toward making your compelling purpose real. And you're likely feeling pretty jazzed and at least a little bit "gulpy." The next order of business, then, is to create a plan for moving forward on your game. Because if you have a Bigger Game and you don't have a game plan, you are "all hat and no cattle," as they say in Texas to describe those dudes who would rather talk about cows than actually lasso one.

A Bigger Game plan is a business plan of sorts. What follows is a game plan tool that you can use to capture the key results you want to create around your compelling purpose – and then to plot out the next moves both for your game and for you, the player. A game plan not only provides a blueprint for what you'll do every day… It also provides the basis for assessing how your game is going and how you are doing at any given moment. Without a game plan, you have no way to chart your progress.

The grid
Meet your key planning tool, the Bigger Game grid. It looks just like the Bigger Game Board, but with all the words wiped off.

Bigger Game Grid

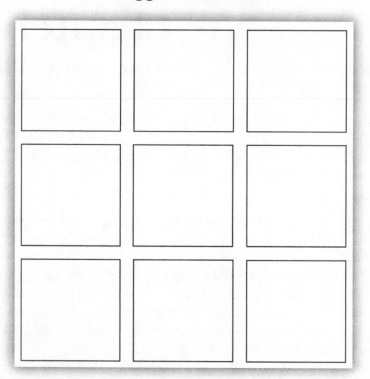

You can use the grid tool to capture all your creative ideas as well as to chart a concrete, step-by-step path toward accomplishing your Bigger Game. You can also use it to *find* your Bigger Game if you haven't got one yet.

The concept of the grid is that you put the main topic in the center and then capture all the important elements in the surrounding squares. The main topic may be your compelling purpose, your Bigger Game, an element of your Bigger Game, or whatever you're working on at the moment. The central concept is to start from the largest piece and "chunk it down."

Creating your game plan requires that you start from the end and the beginning simultaneously. In the beginning is a compelling purpose that rocks your world, along with several great ideas for manifesting it. In the end are the key results or outcomes that will occur when your Bigger Game has been unleashed in your world. Your game plan will bridge the continuum from now until the "end" and beyond. By the way, we'll be walking you through the process of using the grid as we go.

It's important to keep in mind that the alpha and omega of the planning process is about big-picture dreaming. Thoughts about *what's realistic* and *how* have no place here. There's plenty of room for concrete, nuts-and-bolts action items as we move along the bridge between the beginning and the end. But it's the beginning and end that will keep you remembering why it is you want to move heaven and earth to make your Bigger Game real.

Starting from the end...
The end of the planning process comprises the key results you want to create by bringing your Bigger Game to life. In other words, what are the changes you want to see – for your world as well as for you, the player?

Again, you'll want to start from big-picture dreaming based on your compelling purpose. Here's an example: Let's say your purpose is to transform the organizational climate in the workplace so that people bring all of themselves to work every day. Now, stand a year or two out and look at what you've brought about as if it's already happened. Key results of your Bigger Game(s) might include:

- Emotionally intelligent leadership has become a key managerial competency at your company.
- Your company routinely invests in emotional intelligence training for all employees, from new-employee orientation on.
- People generally feel great about each other and about their

bosses. There is a lot of laughter in the halls.
- Your company was just named "Company of the Year."
- Your company's business results have shown radical increases; research attributes the improvement to a friendlier climate.
- Peter Senge and Stephen Covey are teaming up to write a book about your company's climate as a model for "creating corporate greatness" in the 2000s.

Capturing these key results with the grid tool would look something like this:

Key Results

Named "Company of the Year"	Emotionally Intelligent Leadership becomes key	
People feel great and laugh!	**Transform Organizational Climate in my workplace**	Company invests in E.I. training
	Radical increases in business results	Senge/Covey write book about us!

Next, capture the key results for you or your team. Again, stand a few years out as if your game has been accomplished, and design who you've become. Using the example above, perhaps your personal key results would include:

- I have been named Executive Vice President.
- My team and I were profiled in *Fast Company* magazine, which called us "gurus of culture transformation."
- I recently made a keynote address at an international conference on the subject of "employee-first culture change."
- I will be taking my first four-month sabbatical this year to study and help transform the cultures of other major companies.
- I host a "human business" show on CNN.

The player grid looks something like this:

Personal Key Results

If you have not yet identified a specific Bigger Game for your-self and/or your team, the end can be the best place to start. Some-times noticing the key results you'd like to create for your world and for yourself will suggest one or more specific Bigger Games that really excite you.

Starting from the beginning...

Starting from the beginning requires that you back up in the model for a moment. Let's say you've identified your most compelling purpose and possibly one or more vehicles for moving it forward – e.g., a number of possible Bigger Games. You may have chosen a Bigger Game that pulls you the most for now. And you're going to want to capture all those other possible games too, because they represent the game that will come *after* this one and, sometimes, the game that will come *before* this one.

For example, let's say your compelling purpose has to do with creating a sense of urgency around sustainability practices because Planet Earth won't survive if we don't. There are many games you could choose to move you toward this purpose. One way is to choose five nonprofit organizations that focus on sustainability and coach their executive directors on how to increase their impact. That's a Bigger Game, for sure. But what's the game after this one? Maybe to coach the boards of the organizations, to make a presentation at a national conference, to work with the nonprofit to create a national campaign around one or more specific sustain-ability practices, and/or to join forces with other sustainability or-ganizations to lobby for a new national holiday: Sustainability Day!

Please remember to include possible Bigger Games that may seem positively far-fetched in their magnitude. That's just the view from this side of the bridge. As your game grows you, you may be equal to more than you ever dreamed possible. So include ideas like launching a global campaign to institute sustainable practices in every company in the world, or being the go-to person for mak-ing unsustainable practices as abhorrent to the American public as littering. Forget *how* for now.

You want to capture all of these "games after the game" as the foundation of your game plan. Because it's not just the game at hand that has the power to inspire and motivate you; it's also the big picture of your compelling purpose and the many other possible vehicles that can move it forward. You want to be prepared with the next big idea a few months or years from now, when it's time for your game to "morph" to the next iteration.

Along the way, you may find that the gulp your named Bigger Game evokes in you is so big that it makes you freeze. Whether you're actually capable of accomplishing it is immaterial if all the blood drains out of your body at the very thought of it. If your game doesn't energize you, it's not the right game for now – though it could well be the right game in the future. So if you're terrified of enrolling the executive directors of five nonprofits to work with you, you'll want to create some possible "games before the game" – maybe coaching the management team of *one* nonprofit to start with, or standing in front of your local market selling reusable cloth grocery bags every Saturday for a year.

Now, use a grid to capture all of these ideas. Place your most compelling purpose in the center and then fill out possible Bigger Games in the outside squares, including the game you have already chosen (if you have) and others that could come before or after it.

When you look at your new grid, does it awaken the thrill and the kind of gulp that invigorates you? It should. Because you'll want to tape the grids to the wall and return to them again and again to remind you what you're up to in the world when you forget.

Measurability

Remember that your compelling purpose is *what* you want to create and your Bigger Game is *how*. There is *doing* involved. For example, your compelling purpose may be to end world hunger. That's the big-picture dream your soul aches to make real, but it's too big to measure. "Spend the next two years visiting third-world communities to help them leverage their own resources" is a measurable game. "Write a book about that experience and the central concept of sufficiency," as author Lynn Twist did with her book *The Soul of Money*, is the game after the game. Those are her pieces of the dream.

In other words, you want to find a game that is specific and measurable enough so that you can organize it, attract allies, know when you have accomplished it, and know what your next game will be.

Here's another example: Laura Whitworth's compelling purpose was to use co-active coaching skills to give people around the world a way to relate to each other through respect and curiosity rather than from blame or judgment. One way to achieve this is to bring coaching training into the American prison system, as Laura did. The prison project served as a laboratory for taking coaching training into law enforcement, education, politics... the possible games after the prison game are legion.

Crystal ball

If we have implied that there's anything resembling clarity about your future games, please drop that notion. Even if the view from this side of the bridge is pretty clear – this game, then this one, then this even bigger one – it doesn't account for one key factor. Change! Circumstances change and you change, too.

As change occurs, you need to be ready to adapt to new circumstances, new ideas, and accept that your game is changing along the way – even if you're not ready for it to change. In these instances, it is important to keep your compelling purpose in mind. Write your compelling purpose in the center of the Bigger Game grid. Post it on your wall. Speak your compelling purpose to anyone who will listen. As your game changes, making your compelling purpose as clear to yourself as possible will help keep you focused on the bigger picture, even as the sand shifts under your feet.

As you work on your game plan, do it in a way that serves you best, as well as in a way that creates fun for you. Do you work best in a partnership or by having a conversation with someone else? Or do you work best by yourself, in a quiet and comfortable setting? Are you a visual person? We've learned that it helps to actually draw the outcome of your Bigger Game. Create a collage. Use objects that represent it. Be creative. What does it look like? How will people be affected? Lots of happy faces? Cancer-free patients? When the game is successful and out in the world, what will we see?

Okay – you now have a game plan. And you know that it will change as you go. Your Bigger Game grids are completed and hanging on your wall. Now what? The next chapter will help you get started.

Summary

- Once you've named a Bigger Game and/or compelling purpose, the next step is to create a game plan.

- Using the Bigger Game grid, put the name of your game and/or your compelling purpose in the center square and then "chunk it down."

- Creating your game plan requires that you start from the end and the beginning simultaneously.

- In the beginning is a compelling purpose that rocks your world, along with several great ideas for manifesting it.

- In the end are the key results or outcomes that will occur when your Bigger Game has been unleashed in your world.

- Remember that your compelling purpose is *what* you want to create, and your Bigger Game is *how*.

- As change occurs, you need to be ready to adapt to new circumstances, new ideas, and accept that your game is changing along the way – even if you're not ready for it. Keeping your steadfast compelling purpose front and center will help.

Chapter 10
Getting It and Keeping It Going: Investment and Sustainability

In order to arrive at the point where you have named your compelling purpose and/or your Bigger Game, you have probably invested considerable time and attention toward expanding your awareness of your hunger, as well as the field's hunger. You have endured the discomfort of leaving comfort zones. You may have experimented with facing down the gulp, building alliances, and disciplining yourself to assess rather than vote. Now that you've named your game, though, it's time to up the ante on investments – especially in you, the Bigger Game player.

At the same time, it's important to consider the end, even as you are at the very beginning. As you invest in what it will take to get your game off to a good start, start thinking about what it will take to keep your game thriving over time. Think about how to sustain and build your health, energy, and competencies as a game player. And think about how to sustain the momentum and infrastructure of the game itself so that it could go on without you if necessary. Investment and Sustainability are separate elements of the Game Board, yes, yet they are inextricably linked. That's why, in this chapter, we'll be talking about them together.

Investing in yourself, the Bigger Game player

If you already had the competencies to play this game, it would not be a Bigger Game for you. You must develop new capabilities and skills, and expand your capacity to move through the gulp with ease. This doesn't just happen by accident. It's important to prepare yourself as best you can for this venture. And that means investing in you.

The ports of entry for self-investment include:

- Time: You'll need to carve out time to make your Bigger Game happen. This can entail getting help, getting better organized, leaving the comfort zones of time-consuming pleasures that cost your game, and saying "no" to commitments in your life that don't serve your game.

- Action: You'll need to take action, because until you do, your Bigger Game is only a shining thought.

- Money: You'll need to look at your finances and do whatever it takes to make sure you are taking care of yourself as your game moves forward.

- Intention: You need to focus your intention on what you want to create, your Bigger Game.

- Attention: You need to practice putting your attention on the field, assessing what's going on out there, and assessing the soul hunger that resides in you. The discipline of keeping your attention on the field so that you can read where people are and meet them there is a cornerstone of Bigger Game skills – and a key investment area for you.

Clean up, start, stop, and grow

To start playing your Bigger Game, look around your life with
fresh eyes:

- *What do you need to clean up?* This spans everything from tidy-
  ing up and painting your workspace to repairing broken relationships that consume your time and attention, to following through
  on incomplete commitments in your life. It may also necessitate
  getting your affairs in order – making a will at last, buying dis-
  ability insurance, changing the beneficiaries on your life insurance policy – all those loose ends in your life that consume time
  and psychic energy.

- *What do you need to start?* This might include establishing bene-
  ficial new comfort zones such as a program of regular exercise, a
  healthier diet, time set aside each day for reflection or journaling,
  and/or a practice of finding things that make you gulp and doing
  them anyway. (Karaoke, anyone?) You may want to begin attending Toastmasters or networking events in order to augment
  your skills and contacts. You may want to order magazine sub-
  scriptions, books, and/or recordings that will teach you more
  about the realm of your game. You may want to get more sleep
  every night and take that vacation you've been putting off so that
  you can generate more energy and enthusiasm for your game.
  You probably want to start building new strategic alliances that
  serve your game. And you definitely want to start saying the
  name of your Bigger Game out loud, and talking about it in detail
  to anyone and everyone you meet.

- *What do you need to stop?* The biggest stop sign here is around
  comfort zones that have a high cost to your Bigger Game. For
  example, you may need to stop smoking for the sake of your
  energy. To stop watching four hours of TV a night in order to
  free up more time to rest and reflect. To stop procrastinating by
  keeping yourself busy with the minutiae of life (this is a very
  common comfort zone, by the way). To stop indulging in distractions such as shopping or alcohol or complaining. To stop

doing everything all by yourself and invest in some help resources – a cleaning person, bookkeeper, or personal assistant, for example – in order to clear out more space and create more order in your life. You'll definitely want to quit buying into that habitual, critical inner voice that says things like "I can't," "I don't have time," "It's too hard," "I don't know how," and "Failing will kill me." Most of all, you'll want to stop playing the waiting game. I'll wait until my mortgage is paid off. I'll wait until the children are grown. I'll wait until I'm retired and have more time. I'll wait until I really know what I'm doing. Truth is, you can literally wait yourself to death. And we suspect you don't want your tombstone to read: "Was going to do something meaningful... but never got around to it."

- *How do you need to grow?* What rigid patterns of thought or behavior does your Bigger Game ask you to work on? How do you need to evolve emotionally to become ever more aware of how your ego, conditioning, and inner critic run the show? Do you have an emotional support system in place? What is your relationship with failing? Where will you turn when disappointments and failures knock you down? Who is your primary source of emotional support? Who is your backup person when your primary support is unavailable? How are you building resilience and "toughness?" What do you need to do to ensure that you continually improve your capacity to gulp, step through it, recover, and do it all over again?

Sustainability
How does investment differ from sustainability? Investment is about getting something going. Sustainability is about maintaining and building on what's already up and running. Sustainability is essential in two areas. First, you need to do what it takes to sustain you, the Bigger Game player. Second, you need to ensure the sustainability of the game itself so that if you disappear, the game can thrive without you.

Sustaining you, the Bigger Game player

You are an "engine" of your game, so it requires you to sustain yourself. That means you need to keep your health, energy, moods, money, and relationships in good working order, no matter what.

For all too many Americans, the preferred answer to the question "How are you?" is "Busy." Being busy makes us feel useful, important, and visible. The busier we are and the more we work, the more important we are, goes the thinking here. "Busyness" is among the most pervasive and insidious comfort zones in our culture, and it can easily cost you your Bigger Game. Why? Busy gets in the way of self-care, reflection, relation building, and planning. Busy plays hell with strategic thinking and rest. And busy blocks our ability to listen to our soul hunger and be inspired by our compelling purpose.

The challenge, of course, is that a Bigger Game is all about bold action. When you get inspired, you want to tear into the work, advance your compelling purpose, move, move, move.... Great! But watch out...you've just crossed over the line between bold action and mindless busyness. This line is where assessment is essential. You need to notice the bold actions that are filling your waking hours and the extent to which they do or do not serve your game. You need to quiet your mind enough to listen to the field so that your game can tell you the next move to make. You need to notice when your engagement and sense of flow devolve into the insidious comfort zone of gerbil-on-a-wheel busyness.

Busyness for its own sake does not serve you. Nor does zealotry. If you get driven or obsessed, or if you work yourself into a state of exhaustion or burn out, you have probably returned to the comfort zone of busyness, and most likely your Bigger Game has devolved into a self game.

What this means is that you must take good care of yourself for the sake of your Bigger Game. Making sure you take your vacation is not an indulgence – your game demands it. Taking care of yourself may look like meditating daily, working with a personal trainer, scheduling an immutable weekly date night with your partner, getting to bed by 11 PM each night, getting medical and dental checkups on schedule, playing with your friends, and more. You need to continually give yourself the replenishment, training, development, and resources that provide fuel for your success over time.

The Wheel of Life
The Wheel of Life was developed by the Coaches Training Institute for personal and professional coaches to use with their clients. It provides a handy reference point for assessing how you're doing to create sustainability in each of the major areas of your life.

Wheel of Life
Give yourself a 1–10 score for each area of the wheel

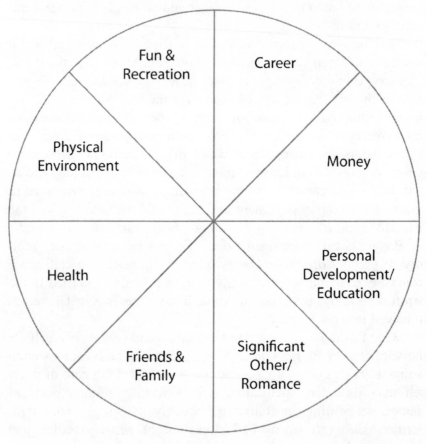

As you look toward sustaining yourself as a Bigger Game player, use this wheel to give yourself a 1-10 score on how you're doing in each area. In those areas where your scores are low, what investments will you make in order to take better care of yourself and your life? You will want to add these actions to your game plan.

And finally, an important part of sustaining yourself for the sake of your Bigger Game is your continued soul hunger and commitment, so it's important to monitor the extent to which your game continues to inspire you. Assessing is critical here. Notice every day where you are in your game and if it still has the power to thrill you when you say it out loud. If it doesn't, how does your game need to change so that you're still as committed as you were on day one? If your game no longer calls you forth and grows you, it doesn't matter how well you are taking care of yourself; it's not your game anymore.

Sustaining your game
There is a paradox here: It is critical for you to sustain yourself because you are an engine of your Bigger Game. And yet, if you become the be-all and end-all of your game, how can it survive beyond you? When you look toward sustaining your game into the future, with or without your continued presence, what is needed?

It is useful to focus your attention on the Game Board elements of Investment and Allies. Do you have co-players who are just as committed to the success of your game as you are? What additional training and expertise do they need to carry the game forward without you? Do you need to invest in a strategic planning retreat for your key players to make sure the game is still big enough to thrive and to keep the team fired up and united? Do you have constituents, clients, sponsors, and other sources of ongoing support? Do you have expert resources in place who know as much as you do about how to maintain and build the infrastructure for your game? What investments do you need to make in building alliances? Have you received enough press coverage to win a widespread audience and recruit new constituents?

The games you play in your life are what create your legacy – the memory of who you were and the power of your contribution that continue long after you are no longer part of the scene. Consider Martin Luther King, for example. King's compelling purpose – I have a dream... of freedom for all – and his Bigger Game of desegregation have burned bright for four decades after his death. We can't be sure that he was deliberately designing his game to be sustainable, but he was very deliberate about recruiting co-players, word-spreaders, voters, supporters, and even enemies in order to make sure that the American people would never, ever forget the compelling purpose of freedom for all.

Important, not urgent

When you are immersed in the demands of your game, sustainability considerations can seem secondary – important, yes, but something that can be put off until you have time to give it your undivided attention. It's like the task of making a will. Yes, of course you need one, but you don't need to get it done this very day. Beware of this comfort zone. Called "reactivity" and akin to "busyness for its own sake," it is very common in a business world that is increasingly measured by quarter-on-quarter results. And yet, the reactive mentality that has us put out the fires of today without tending the flame for tomorrow has spelled the doom of many a grand enterprise before yours.

Management guru Stephen Covey asserts that business people perform four fundamental types of activities based on the factors of importance and urgency. These include:

1) Important and urgent
2) Important and not urgent
3) Not important and urgent
4) Not important and not urgent

"Important" activities are what make an organization – or a Bigger Game – successful. The challenge is that urgency usually takes precedence over importance. In other words, handling today's emergencies often demands more immediate attention than something that can be delayed until tomorrow. That's well and good when the task represents something that is "important and urgent." However, planning for the future is one of those functions that is "important and *not* urgent." Most people would agree that devoting attention to future sustainability is vitally important to any endeavor, but you don't have to create one right this minute when you have so many other pressing concerns... Or do you?

Here's the current reality for many of us: We're busy, and we get caught up in what we have to do each day. Consequently, we play the "if only" game – if only we get this task done, then we'll sit down, assess what's needed, and make a plan. The trouble is, there are always more fires to douse. In truth, the only way out of this reactive orientation is to step out of the cycle, notice what is and is not important, and plan how to use our precious time to best advantage. It doesn't matter what's on the To Do list. Nothing is more important than assessing and planning. Your very legacy depends on it.

Your game demands it
When it comes to investment and sustainability, there's a lot to pay attention to. Self-care. The mental discipline to think strategically rather than reactively. All those workshops and seminars to attend, allies to recruit, assistants to hire and train, vacations to plan, the minefields of busyness to monitor.... How is a Bigger Game player to sort it all out?

Let's make it simple. Job #1 for every Bigger Game player is to listen to your game. Put your attention on the field. Notice that you are part of the field and include yourself in your attention out there. Assess where you are. Assess what's needed now. Do that. Then repeat the cycle. If you have a game that inspires you and feeds the hunger of your soul, it has the power to pull you toward what you need to do. You don't have to force it. Just allow yourself to be led. When you allow your game to guide and inform you, you'll have plenty to do in the areas of investment and sustainability. And you'll move boldly in a life-giving flow that keeps the fire burning bright without burning out you or your game.

Summary

- Investment is what it takes to get your game off to a good start, while sustainability is what it takes to keep your game going and growing over time.

- Investment starts with investing in you, the Bigger Game player. Expect to invest your time, money, intention, attention, and action in your game. What do you need to clean up? Start doing? Stop doing? Where do you need to grow emotionally? What would taking superb care of yourself look like?

- You are an engine of your Bigger Game. To sustain it, you need to sustain yourself. That means you need to keep your health, energy, moods, money, and relationships in good working order – and resist the insidious comfort zone of "busyness."

- Sustaining your Bigger Game so that it can go forward without you requires strategic thinking around continuing investments and building alliances. These activities are all-important but "not urgent." It's essential to resist the comfort zone of "reactivity," or extinguishing today's fires at the expense of your game's future.

- If you are diligent about keeping your attention on the field, your game will lead you to what's needed next and help you steer clear of the traps of busyness and reactivity.

Chapter 11
Allies

A   *lly*: to unite or form a connection between; one that is associated with another as a helper

Alliance: an association to further the common interests of the members

A Bigger Game, by definition, is too big to be played by yourself. If you can accomplish your game on your own, it probably is not a Bigger Game. That doesn't mean it isn't important and valuable; it's just not a Bigger Game.

Reflect on your compelling purpose for a moment and let all considerations of "how" fall away. If you had access to all the influence, money, time, manpower, and other resources in the world, how big would you want your game to be? What kind of impact could it have?

You have a choice here. You can "think big" and then edit your vision so that it is realistic given your current resources. Or you can "think big" and recruit the resources you need to make it happen in all its amazing glory. The latter is what allies are for.

As we've said, a Bigger Game is by the people and for the people. The more people supporting you in your game and playing along with you, the greater the wallop your game will pack. And incidentally, you'll have infinitely more fun! Maybe the Marlboro Man enjoys galloping around by himself with only cows for company, but Bigger Game players enjoy the company of humans, know how to play well with others, and understand that two heads are better than one – and a thousand heads are exponentially better yet. Truly, if you want to make an enormous splash, you can't go it alone. And why would you even want to?

Your allies include people who are wildly supportive of you and your game. They include co-players, people who make your Bigger Game their own. They include experts who can compensate for your gaps in skills, knowledge, and resources and free your time to do what you're best at. And they even include people who disagree with you or resist what you're doing. Your allies also include the people served by your game – your prospects, clients, audience, participants, and/or beneficiaries. Your job is to identify your "dream team" of allies, recruit them, design them to be optimal partners, lead the charge, and keep redesigning your alliances along the way as your Bigger Game evolves and your needs change.

Ideally, your allies really know you. They know your strengths, your weaknesses, and your blind spots. They will let you know when you've strayed off the path, and they really know how to call you forth. But allies represent a force far more potent than merely your personal cheerleading squad. In a game that's by the people and for the people, you need to connect with powerful movers and shakers who can help you spread the word and make things happen. The informal "Six Degrees of Separation Rule" declares that it never takes more than six human connections to link you directly to any person on the planet. For example, if I wanted to reach Robert Redford with a script, I could contact a friend who knows somebody who knows somebody who knows somebody who knows somebody who knows Redford personally – and can deliver my script into his hands. As a Bigger Game player, then, you want to recruit a network of allies that creates a hugely leveraged ripple of impact.

The right people, the right time, the right message

Your allies constitute the network that literally connects you to the world; at the same time, they bring their own unique strengths and contributions to your party. In his best-selling book on social contagion, *The Tipping Point*, author Malcolm Gladwell points out that catalyzing significant social change requires a surprisingly small critical mass; all it takes is the right people at the right time with the right message.

The right time and the right message are your specialties as the Bigger Game player. You have identified what is needed, read the hunger in the field, and given birth to a purpose so compelling you can't say no to it. According to Gladwell, the people you need to help leverage your message and its timing include mavens, salespeople, and networkers. Mavens are experts who know everything about everything – and love to share what they know. They're the ones who do extensive research on pretty much everything so that you don't have to. Next come salespeople, who have such marvelous people skills and are so deft at packaging messages that they are almost impossible to resist. And finally, Gladwell points to the networkers, those people who cross social domains to link influence-leaders in many different fields – and spread your message like wildfire.

When you're thinking about creating a dream team of allies – because that's what's next on the Game Board – you'll want a few mavens, salespeople, and networkers in your court. There are lots of other kinds of allies you'll want to consider, too. Let's take a look.

Identifying your dream team

Your allies may include supporters, clients, teammates, co-players, bosses, family members, managers, schoolmates, city council members, professors, coaches, gurus, ministers, rabbis, mentors, experts, reporters, competitors, the media, naysayers, and your next-door neighbor, to name a few. It is critical for you to identify the kinds of allies you need to carry your game forward as well as the specific people you want to fill these roles. Before you begin naming names, however, let's take a look at some of the major kinds of allies we've identified and the function they serve vis-à-vis your Bigger Game. You're likely to notice considerable cross-over among categories, by the way.

Friends/listeners: This category includes people who don't need much recruiting. They already know and love you, and if it matters to you, it matters to them. They are glad to listen to you and will comfort you when you need it. They will cheer you on, cheer you up, and cheer your victories. When you're just getting your Bigger Game going and need to say it out loud, these allies can give you invaluable practice and feedback. As is true with all your allies, you will need to train your friends and listeners. If they've known you for a long time, they are accustomed to the way you have been, so they may be inclined to accept your excuses and collude with your comfort zones. Teach them to refuse to take "I don't wanna" for an answer. Ask them for encouragement, not collusion, when you're hesitating to try something that scares you. And ask them to keep calling you forth to nothing less than your best.

Prospects/constituents/clients: These are the people your game exists to serve. If you don't get them on board, you don't have a Bigger Game. Once they truly understand what you're up to and join forces with you, they will be your staunchest supporters because there's so much in it for them.

Co-players: Every Bigger Game has to have at least one of these; without co-players, your game has no sustainability. These partners have as much ownership in your Bigger Game as you do. They share your hunger and compelling purpose, and are investing and gulping right alongside you. If anything should happen to you, your game will go on without you because of these allies. They are precious.

Champions: These allies think you're just great, as your friends and listeners do, but they also think your Bigger Game is just great, that it has to happen, and that you're the one to do it – and they'll remind you of this when you forget. They care fiercely that you and your game be wildly successful, and they don't much care how you accomplish it as long as you do.

Coach/mentor: This ally is a professional who is well-versed in the Bigger Game model and is committed to shepherd you through the process with rigor to help you make your game real. A coach or mentor has expertise and will provide advice, as needed, yet the ownership of the game remains with you, the player. Your Bigger Game coach or mentor is usually among the most powerful champions imaginable.

Expert resources: Your Bigger Game requires skills that you don't already possess, yet you by no means need to do everything yourself. You'll frequently be faced with a choice: Will it grow me to learn how to do this myself, or is my time better spent elsewhere? When the answer is "Farm it out," the modern-day equivalent of the butcher, the baker, and the candlestick maker is your accountant, attorney, publicist, technology geek, grant writer, project manager, copywriter, personal trainer, organizer, personal assistant, and sales team. Your expert resources are all those people you recruit to handle important functions for your game that don't represent a good use of your time.

Spirit/nature: No matter what religious tradition you follow, the practice of quieting your mind, opening your heart, and connecting with nature and/or spirit, as you know it, is a great source of inspiration and comfort for Bigger Game players. "God," as you understand the concept, can be one of your most powerful allies of all.

Investors: Mothers Against Drunk Driving (MADD) found "angel sponsors" who provided funding for many years of operation and enabled the organization's rapid growth. Not all Bigger Games require money to succeed, but most do. Financial investment can be a cornerstone in starting and sustaining Bigger Games.

Volunteers: Board members, fund-raisers, telephone canvassers, door knockers, envelope stuffers... volunteers provide influence and needed functions at a price your game can afford.

Naysayers/enemies/competitors: Those who are not on your side can serve as your allies in several useful ways. They can stiffen your resolve and inspire you to prove them wrong – "Hell no, you're not going to tell me I can't!" When naysayers point to flaws in your game plan, you have the opportunity to correct them while sharpening your strategic thinking. And competitors can drive you to meet a higher bar than you would have without their example.

Come in and get me: All allies are important, but none more so than those who commit to come in and get you when you're overwhelmed, when you retreat into old comfort zones, and when you lose faith in yourself or your game. What you're doing is not easy, after all. You care passionately about your compelling purpose, and yet you get tired or discouraged or sidetracked and forget what matters most. Your *come in and get me* ally never forgets. In service of your compelling purpose, he or she won't let you hide or lie to yourself. And when you tell them to buzz off, they refuse to go until you can see your game clearly once again and locate yourself on the Game Board. If you do not create a couple of *come in and get me* allies for yourself, you are in denial about the human tendency to retreat into comfort zones.

Heroes/Sheroes: It's not necessary for you to know someone personally to have them as a powerful ally. Think of those people who have inspired you most in your life – from your 6th-grade teacher to Abraham Lincoln to Jack Welch to Oprah Winfrey to Bill Gates to Bono. Let their example inspire you. If they are still alive, write them a letter and tell them what your Bigger Game is about. Who knows? Your heroes/sheroes on pedestals may become your hands-on helpers as well.

Look around. Your potential allies are everywhere. It's time now for you to identify the kinds of allies you want – and start naming names.

Leading the way
Identifying both the kinds of allies you need and specific people

who fill the bill is the first part of your allies strategy. Now it's time to start recruiting, designing, and training them. You have two precious gifts to offer prospective allies: you the Bigger Game player and your Game itself, backed by your compelling purpose. Depending on whom you're approaching, choose which of the two to put forth first, but be sure to offer both.

Recruiting allies, designing your relationship with them, and training them in the needs of your game will call on your leadership skills like nobody's business. This is collaborative influence in action. You must earn your allies' trust, inspire them, call forth the best in them, and empower them in the service of your Bigger Game.

Here's where to start:

- Think *big* when you're framing your game. Instead of tailoring your vision to accommodate what's "realistic," dare to go for what's impossible – and then recruit the allies who can help take you there.
- You must see where you honestly need help and learn to ask for it. And then get better at asking for help.
- You must meet your allies where they are before you point them where you want to go – and then become skilled at dancing with whatever happens next.
- You must become good at getting "over there" with others and giving them your complete attention so that they feel heard; this is a cornerstone of building trust.
- You must become good at inspiring and motivating people.
- You must recognize the greatness in others and tell them so.
- You must empower others as leaders.
- The impact of your communication is revealed in the response you get; if the response is not what you want, say it another way.
- You must build your resilience and your capacity to assess without voting, so that when things don't go your way or your own impact dismays you, you can recover rapidly to the needs of the field and your people.
- Most of all, you must see your allies as fellow human beings who are just as unique, talented, passionate, and powerful as you are.

You must see what they care about and help them align their concerns with what you're up to. Remember, if you see your allies as objects – as vehicles, barriers, or irrelevant to your game – you will find yourself going it alone... and your game will fail.

Your "allies" strategy
By identifying the kinds of allies you need and a few specific names, you have begun to implement an allies strategy that will help you create the team of people who will be your co-players, cheerleaders, investors, administrative resources, mavens, salespeople, and networkers.

Forming an "allies" strategy looks something like this:

- Identify the kinds of allies you need to move your Bigger Game forward.

- Identify specific people to recruit as your allies in each category. A note here: Start from the assumption that anyone on the planet would love to help you move your Bigger Game forward, including presidents, kings, rock stars, captains of industry, and the pope. That means choosing the best person for the assignment, whether you currently have access to that person or not. You can always go to Plan B later if you need to, but you might as well dream big to start.

- Recruit your allies. Your adoring grandfather as a cheerleader? Piece of cake. The governor of your state? Ummm, yes, recruiting some of the prospects on your allies list elicits a gulp and calls for some mighty bold action. That's as it should be. You want power players on your team.

Now, where do you need to invest in order to reach these people and bring them into the fold?

- You'll want to be so steeped in your compelling purpose that you would do virtually anything to make it happen. It's a good idea to practice speaking your compelling purpose to others, because that will usually be the most powerful draw for the power players. Remember, you're asking on behalf of your game, not yourself.

• You're not alone in wanting to do something meaningful with your life. You are offering prospective allies the gift of an opportunity to rock the world, and they want to do that as much as you do (though not necessarily in the way you want to rock it). So a major part of your recruiting effort has to do with connecting with the hunger of their souls.

• Meet-Point-Dance: Once you've put your compelling purpose out there, determine how the other person is receiving it. What's going on over there? What's their hunger? Ideally, you want to create an alliance of enlightened self-interest where both parties are nourished by the association. Find out from them what it would take for that to be true.

• Be very specific about what you're requesting. "I want your help" is too vague. "I want you to introduce me to major media contacts in ten cities" lets them know the extent of the involvement you envision and how much of their time it will take.

• Get used to taking "no" for an answer... and don't take "no" for an answer. The more often you hear "no" and get to practice assessing without voting on what it means about you, the easier it becomes for you to invite the people you want on your team. That said, "no" doesn't always mean "no." Maybe they don't want to be involved in the capacity you envision, but they're willing to help you in some other way, or connect you with other prospective allies. Maybe it requires a second conversation, and a third and fourth, as they see you putting your money where your heart is. Hang in there; you're doing this for your game.

• Ask your allies for help in recruiting new allies. It's often easier to contact someone if someone else has introduced you. Ask your allies who they know – or who they know that might know the person you want to reach. You'll be stunned at the richness of their Rolodex resources.

• Design and train your allies. To design allies well, it is important to teach them how to give us what we need to succeed at all levels. You'll be asking for different kinds of support from different people, and you need to make your requests and expectations clear right from the start. For example, you want to train your "come in and get me" ally to check in when they haven't heard from you for a week or so, to help you rediscover where you are on the Game Board, to refuse to collude with your retreat into comfort zones, and to stand firm when you try to shoo them away. You want your bookkeeper to give you weekly, monthly, or quarterly reports – whatever works best for you. Make clear requests and ask for direct feedback on what's working and what isn't along the way. And be prepared to redesign continually as circumstances change, doors close, new doors open, and your allies reveal new possibilities and capabilities.

• Recognize and reward your allies: Make sure that what you appreciate about your allies does not go without saying. Tell them frequently and specifically what you appreciate about them and their contribution to your shared Bigger Game. Bestow credit wherever it's due. If you put your attention on acknowledging and recognizing your allies, you'll get all the recognition you deserve in return, without having to ask for it. When it's about credit for you, by the way, it becomes an ego game.

When you have surrounded yourself with a dream team of allies – all of whom have invested in your Bigger Game and bring ideas and resources of their own to the field, your game not only becomes infinitely more doable; it also becomes more expansive.

Your allies and changing circumstances deliver more possibilities, promising tangents to explore, the next challenge and the one after that. This is a normal and joyful process we call "morphing," as your Bigger Game evolves to keep pace with what the field needs now and who you have become.

Summary

• The more people supporting you in your game and playing along with you, the greater the wallop your game will pack. And the more fun you'll have.

• Your allies may include supporters, clients, teammates, co-players, bosses, family members, managers, schoolmates, city council members, professors, coaches, gurus, ministers, rabbis, mentors, experts, reporters, competitors, the media, naysayers, and your next door neighbor, to name a few. It is critical for you to identify the kinds of allies you need to carry your game forward as well as the specific people you want to recruit. Think big!

• All allies are important, but none more so than those who commit to *come in and get you* when you're overwhelmed, when you retreat into old comfort zones, and when you lose faith in yourself or your game.

• Recruiting and training allies and maintaining these relationships call for all your leadership skills.

• Your allies strategy includes these elements:

  - Identify the kinds of allies you need.
  - Name specific people to fill these roles.
  - Recruit your allies by inspiring them with your compelling purpose, making specific requests, and Meet-Point-Dance.
  - Design the alliances and be prepared to redesign en route.
  - Recognize and reward your allies.

Chapter 12
Morphing Your Bigger Game

"**M**orph" is the word we use to describe the process of organic evolution that characterizes every Bigger Game. It is no exaggeration to say that human civilization, as we know it, is a product of Bigger Games that have morphed. The process looks something like this: History-makers hunger for something, and the confluence of time, place, and circumstances dictates a corresponding hunger in the field. The result is a compelling purpose, a game, a plan, allies, and the powerful thrust forward. And then... circumstances change. Wars are declared. A new ruler is installed. Famine, drought, or exceptionally rich harvests affect the needs of the people. New opportunities open up. New barriers rise to thwart forward momentum or create detours. New allies offer hitherto unimagined ideas and capabilities. Or, the Bigger Game is actually accomplished... and it's time to move on to the next game that will ink a thumbprint on the world while it grows its players. This is pretty much how the course of human history has been charted so far.

Repeat Bigger Game players are no strangers to the phenomenon of morphing. In fact, they live to morph! Consider classic entrepreneurs like British innovator Sir Richard Branson, who is best known for his Virgin brand of over 360 companies: airlines, record stores, humanitarian initiatives, and numerous other business ventures. Or Paul Newman, movie star turned food entrepreneur. Or Ted Turner, whose serial Bigger Games are as disparate as buffalo ranching, America Cup yachting, the first all-news cable TV network (CNN), a cable network that showcases classic movies, and fielding a pro baseball team that has won the World Series. Or aerospace engineer Burt Rutan, who is most famous for his design of the record-breaking Voyager, the first plane to fly around the world without stopping or refueling, and is now noted for his originality in designing energy-efficient aircraft. Or filmmaker/author Michael Moore, whose Bigger Game of "waking people up" uses documentary films and books to expose everything from gun control practices to politicians' hidden agendas.

Simply put, all Bigger Games morph. Or they aren't Bigger Games. Within days or weeks of naming your game, it is likely that it will begin to change or evolve – and so will you. What's this about? Does it mean you didn't get it right the first time? Should you stick with your original game and the strategy you created for it? The answers here are "no" and "no." The fact that your game morphs is natural, normal, and pretty darned exciting. It is supposed to morph. If it doesn't, it either isn't big enough for you – or you're holding on way too tight.

Alice Coles' Bigger Game(s)

Let's take a look at a series of Bigger Games that followed a classic morphing pattern. They represent the recent history of Alice Coles, who we introduced earlier in this book.

Alice Coles had lived all her life in Bayview, Virginia, a dilapidated, rural town characterized by ramshackle dwellings – many of them burned out – with no electricity or running water. Nothing had changed in Bayview for several generations; the people were accustomed to living in squalor (an example of when a comfort zone has nothing to do with comfort), and nobody was pressing for change. In 1995, though, the state announced plans to build a maximum-security prison on the property right next door to

Bayview. For Alice Coles, this was the last straw. As she recounted in a story on *60 Minutes*, Coles "opened [her] mouth right then and said, 'No, I'm not going to take this.'"

Bigger Game #1: Defeat the prison project. Alice Coles, then a 45-year-old single mother with a high school education, became a vocal opponent of the prison and rallied her neighbors to the cause; together, they lobbied to defeat the prison – and succeeded. Alice took a look at what they had accomplished by breaking out of their generations-old comfort zone of silent resignation, and she said, "If I can defeat the prison, why live like this?" Alice was exercising the Bigger Game element called "assess," by the way, an invaluable tool in the morphing process.

At that moment, Alice's next Bigger Game was born with the formation of Bayview Citizens for Social Justice. Their aim was to create decent housing for the people of their little town. And Alice Coles was among a cadre of eight leaders who led the charge and shared a common Bigger Game.

The coalition's scope was very broad, and they were starting from scratch. To move forward, they had to blast out of comfort zone after comfort zone, because there was no part of this game that they already knew how to play. They started by polling all residents of the Bayview community to create a vision for the future. Then, they needed to learn how to organize, create a budget, raise funds, and lobby the state and federal government for support. Early on, the group found an ally and co-player in architect and college professor Maurice Cox, who helped them orchestrate a community-wide cleanup effort that included demolishing the worst of the burned-out shacks. Morale soared as the debris of many decades was carted away to reveal fresh earth.

When progress seemed to be at a standstill, Alice thought to enlist civil rights leaders to publicize Bayview as a bastion of slavery, a move that attracted the attention of politicians and funding sources. This move resulted in the funding of $4 million from the State of Virginia, $4 million from the US government, and $2 million from private sources.

Now powered by $10 million in capital, Alice's Bigger Game morphed yet again, this time into a construction project of massive proportions. The gulp was huge; no one in the community had a clue how to manage any building project, much less the rebuilding of an entire town. Again, Alice recruited a powerful ally in the person of project manager Anabola Ajayay. The project became his Bigger Game, too, as it had for so many of the residents of Bayview.

In October 2003, the citizens of Bayview, Virginia, packed their belongings and moved into their new homes. The move represented a physical distance of just 100 feet or so. In terms of civic pride and personal growth, however, the distance they traveled to turn on their own faucets for the first time was immeasurable. As a result of their series of Bigger Games, Alice Coles and her co-players had become vastly more empowered and skilled human beings as they took responsibility for creating a better way to live.

The morphing process

Let's take a closer look at the process by which Bigger Games morph.

You take to the Bigger Game playing field when you explore your deepest soul hunger and find where it intersects with what's needed "out there" to create a purpose so compelling that you just can't say no. You name your Bigger Game, field your team, and start moving forward. At the beginning, the whole thing is a bit theoretical because you haven't been informed by experience yet. As you walk along the path, though, landmarks begin to stand out – and then they begin to change. In fact, the view begins to alter the moment you name your game and take your first bold action. Once the view begins to shift, the specific thrusts of your most compelling purpose become clearer. At this point, it's useful to re-examine the name of your game and see if it still serves what you are up to now. In some cases, a new game and a new name may emerge mere days after naming the last one.

What determines how and when your game morphs is the all-important element of "assess." What is my game? Does it still support the change I want to create in my world? Is it still big enough to challenge and grow the person I'm becoming now? How is my game going? How am I doing? What needs to happen next?

Over time, all Bigger Games will morph. Pitfalls will trip you up. Synchronicity comes into play; providence provides. As a player, you need to choreograph the dance between your game/strategy and opportunities/barriers as they arise. This is, by the way, a logical extension of Meet-Point-Dance – only you're dancing with your world as well as the people in it. What will slow or stop you is failing to notice that your game wants to morph while you are clinging to a game that has run out of juice.

Strategic versus organic
The ability to think strategically is a good thing, right? After all, who ever got anywhere without a good, solid plan. In some respects, this reasoning is quite true. Plans are indispensable tools! At the same time, though, thinking analytically, planning things out, and getting ourselves attached to the plan represents a huge comfort zone for many human beings. What happens then is that the field changes, economic circumstances change, and we become so attached to our plan that we don't even notice what's happening out there. In other words, attachment to a strategic plan can be a comfort zone that keeps us from seeing what wants to change.

Notice we're not saying that the fact of having a strategic plan is a comfort zone. It's great to have a plan. It is our attachment to the plan that gets us in trouble and keeps us from seeing what needs to happen next.

A Bigger Game morphs organically. It will unfold in a natural way if we are alert to notice what's happening and what's needed now. Our job is simply to stay awake and notice. Here's an important clue that something needs to change: If your game is feeling like really hard work – a slog through mud – then it probably isn't inspiring you anymore and it's time to refocus your strategy and create the next draft of your strategic plan. A Bigger Game shouldn't feel hard. Focused, yes. Absorbing, yes. Challenging, yes. But not hard.

An important piece of finding what wants to happen next is to keep looking out into the field rather than down at the plan on your desk – or at your own navel. A Bigger Game that doesn't morph is a self-game that no longer meets the needs of the field.

If month after month goes by and your Bigger Game is not morphing, pay attention. If you and your game are truly evolving, you should be seeing new opportunities. Of course, we all march at a different pace, but if your game is three years old and no morphing has occurred yet, there's something you're not seeing.

Morphing the player: assess, assess, assess

As you know, the assessment process has two parts: *How is my game going?* and *How am I doing?* Let's look at that latter element for a moment.

Here are some of the questions you should be asking yourself:

• In the process of playing this game, who have I become?
• What capacities and capabilities do I have now that I didn't have three months ago?
• How flexible have I become?
• How quickly have I learned to recover from setbacks?
• How clear-eyed and "realistic" have I learned to be without sacrificing one iota of my dream?
• How am I doing with making the distinction between assessing and voting?
• How am I moving toward my compelling purpose?
• How hard am I working?
• What are my blind spots?
• Where do I need to invest now?

When you are a few months into your game, you've probably had some opportunities to fail and recover. (We're defining failing here as going after a specific impact and achieving a different one; there is huge learning in the gap between what you were aiming for and what you actually got.) If you haven't failed, by the way, your game isn't big enough for you. And what have you learned from failing? What needs calibrating? Who are you now and what do you want to invest in next?

By the way, when you are assessing where you've failed and what you've learned from it, please don't go it alone. Remember, your comfort zones will be activated and your blind spots are called "blind" for a reason – if you could already see them, you'd do something about them. It's invaluable, then, to have an ally to help you assess, someone who can help you determine:

• What happened here?
• What do I need to cultivate in myself?
• What needs to happen next?
• Who have I become in the process of getting here?

Sometimes, in the process of assessing, you'll find that your game is still right on target, and yet it's no longer big enough for you. An important part of morphing, then, is to be sure you have allies and co-players who are committed to keeping the game going when it's time for you to move on.

Every element morphs
Morphing occurs at the macro level with the game itself and with you, the player. And morphing happens at the micro level in every square on the Bigger Game Board, too. Let's cruise around the playing field for a moment and take a look.

Comfort zones can morph at a breathtaking speed. For example, when you blast out of a comfort zone that doesn't serve you and create a new pattern of behavior, the new behavior itself becomes a comfort zone as soon as you've repeated it a couple of times – and becomes the next habit you'll want to be blasting out of, more often than not.

Your hunger morphs as you learn more about the field and more about what you're capable of accomplishing. When your attention is attuned to what matters to you, the learning curve is steep and rich. And because Bigger Game players think bigger and bigger all the time, you may find yourself hungering for what was unimaginable only a few months back.

Although a compelling purpose usually remains as constant as the North Star, circumstances can impel you to manifest your purpose in a different realm. For example, the reason behind Laura Whitworth's compelling purpose to bring coaching skills to prison inmates was "They just don't know how." In the midst of her long battle with cancer, though, "They just don't know how" was shaped and flavored by the schism between Western and alternative approaches to treating the disease, and her Bigger Game – or at least one of them – was to integrate treatment into truly patient-centered care.

The gulp morphs constantly, because once you've plunged into what used to scare you, it doesn't scare you any longer and it's time to up the ante. The form of your investment morphs constantly as you identify what you need in order to prepare for whatever comes next in your unfolding game. Allies morph, too, as your game unfolds and you find you need to recruit new capabilities to match the needs of your game. Allies also morph as your allies come to own your game as much as you do – and bring their own ideas and skills to the party.

The elements of your game morph constantly, and at different speeds, in different directions. Morphing can be messy, chaotic, fluid. That's why you have to keep assessing where you are, every single day. You don't want to be waking up three weeks from now and be blindsided by obstacles and/or opportunities you failed to notice. We don't want this to happen – but it will! You want to do everything you can to keep the blindsiding to a minimum.

Remember, there are no hard and fast rules here. Whatever empowers you to keep stepping into your game with both feet is just right. If your compelling purpose morphs 25 times and you remain a Bigger Game player, hurray! Whatever it takes.

The games we play design who we are becoming
Points of entry into the Bigger Game include "Who do I want to become?" and "What is the game that will design that person I aspire to be?" When we say no to business as usual and push ourselves to do what we don't know how to do, we experience discomfort. We may experience failure, too. And we will definitely move toward becoming the person we aspire to be. This pursuit uses all we've got and asks for more. No doubt about it, stretching ourselves is challenging.

At the same time, stretching ourselves is probably the biggest fun a human being can possibly have. In his seminal book, *Flow*, Mihaly Csikszentmihalyi discusses the evolutionary benefits of the flow experience, which involves engaging in activities that are beyond your current reach but within your grasp when you stretch. "Flow activities lead to growth and discovery," he says. "One cannot enjoy doing the same thing at the same level for long. We grow either bored or frustrated, and then the desire to enjoy ourselves again pushes us to stretch our skills or to discover new opportunities for using them."

Celebrating success

Let's say you actually finish the Bigger Game you've been playing. The change is complete. Your thumbprint is all over it. Wahoo! Now what? You have the capacity to go bigger. You have new opportunities, a wider network of allies. It's time to replenish your energy and begin to let your hunger build. What's next?

When your game ends, it is essential to sustainability that you pause to celebrate who you have become, what your game has accomplished, and how your capacity has grown. Celebration is important for its own sake, of course. And it is a key piece of owning who you are now and the territory you occupy so that "jet lag" thinking about who you used to be does not become a factor in looking toward what's next. For example, maybe you've been wondering how to connect with Oprah when, in reality, you've become the person that Oprah is looking to connect with herself.

Celebrating who you are now is a huge element in moving you toward the "game after the game," the one that had you pulling the covers up over your head in terror just a year ago.

Are you ready to play?! Have at it!

Summary

- If your Bigger Game doesn't begin to morph early on, your game probably isn't big enough for you.

- A strategic plan is a good thing, and yet attachment to a strategic plan can become an insidious comfort zone. As a player, you need to choreograph the dance between your game/strategy and opportunities/barriers as they arise. This is, by the way, a logical extension of meet, point, dance – only you're dancing with your world as well as the people in it.

- Assessment – of how the game is going and how you are doing as the player – is the key to responding to what wants to happen next.

- If you, the player, haven't failed, your game isn't big enough for you. What have you learned from failing? What needs calibrating? Who have you become and what do you want to invest in next?

- "Playing a Bigger Game designs who you want to become" is the foundation of the Bigger Game.

- When you complete a game, it is an essential part of sustainability to celebrate who you have become because it informs you of what you're capable of doing next.

Section Four
Inspiring Bigger Game Stories

This section offers a sampling of the myriad Bigger Games that are being played all around you. Some you'll already know about. Others you won't. Now that you know what Bigger Games are, you'll start to notice them everywhere! These stories are meant to spike your imagination toward what's possible when ordinary people set their hearts on extraordinary games. And remember, it's not as important to know the name of your game... it's more important to be a Bigger Game *player* – actively working the Bigger Game Board.

Bigger Game examples of *No, not that!*
Sometimes our hunger is aroused by tragedy, loss, or outrage in the field. Drunk drivers killing children. Discrimination against people of color. World terrorism. Women dying of breast cancer. No, not that! This must never happen again! Our hunger becomes a wake-up call to action. The following are Bigger Game examples that were created from the hunger of *No, not that!*

Wynona Ward/abused women advocate
In Montpelier, Vermont, Wynona Ward, who was raised by an abusive father, drives into the countryside to help abused women pack, flee, and begin to reclaim their lives. Once a trucker, Wynona is now a lawyer and heads the anti-abuse organization Have Justice, Will Travel.

Erin Brockovich/pollution
Erin Brockovich worked as a K-Mart management trainee after college, but quit to enter beauty pageants. In 1993, working as a legal clerk with no formal law school education, the single mother was instrumental in constructing a case against the $28 billion Pacific Gas & Electric Company of California. The case alleged contamination of drinking water with hexavalent chromium in the southern California town of Hinkley; it was settled in 1996 for some $333 million. Brockovich then went on to participate in other anti-pollution lawsuits. Brockovich's efforts have been so effective that a major motion picture was made about her, starring Julia Roberts, who won an Academy Award for her title role. Today, Erin Brockovich is a star in her own right – a shining example of how ordinary people can do extraordinary things when their compelling purpose is strong enough.

Al Gore/global warming awareness
At the pinnacle of his long career in politics, former vice president Al Gore made a hotly contested run for the White House as the Democratic candidate in 2000. He never quite found his voice during that campaign. But he sure has found it in his next incarnation as a

five-star general in the war against global warming.

Gore has always been hungry to get the word out about the damage we have done to the global climate and the role we can play in stemming it. And in 2006, he became Hollywood's improbable darling with his climate-change film, *An Inconvenient Truth*, which has raked in some $40 million in ticket sales and had a long stint on the New York Times bestseller list for the film's companion book. In so doing, Al Gore has reframed the green debate in a way no political figure ever did before. He has alarmed and inspired millions of people to take much more responsibility in addressing the global warming crisis created in this generation.

Patty Wetterling/children abduction advocacy

Patty Wetterling was a junior high math teacher and a soccer mom in the small town of St. Joseph, Minnesota, when, on October 22, 1989, her life changed forever. On that day, her 11-year-old son Jacob was riding his bike home from renting a movie when he and two other boys were accosted in the street by a masked gunman. The man told two of them to run away. Jacob remained with the man... and has never been seen since. Subsequently, Patty Wetterling became a fierce national advocate for child safety; her nonprofit organization, the Jacob Wetterling Foundation, is the main reason that missing children began appearing on the side of milk cartons. Through her foundation, she has secured protections for child safety and pushed through programs to protect children from abduction. Based on the platform of protecting the safety of children and families, Wetterling has also become a major political player in Minnesota, running for US Congress in the fall of 2005.

Jack Raney/seeking the cure for the West Nile virus

Soon after 47-year-old Los Angeles bricklayer Jack Raney recovered from the West Nile infection that left him comatose, he jumpstarted a campaign against the disease that had stolen far too much of his life.

He lobbied California Governor Arnold Schwarzenegger for more West Nile funding, helped public health officials promote a speedy new way to test infected birds (which transmit the virus to mosquitoes that in turn infect people), and joined a small cadre of citizens dedicated to grassroots projects that put a public face on the disease.

Allies in Raney's cause include graduate student, tae kwon do black belt, and motorcycle enthusiast Mitch Coffman of Lafayette, Louisiana, who started a nonprofit called the West Nile Virus Survivors Foundation to provide information about the illness through its Web site. "I don't want to be anybody's hero," said Coffman to Associated Press reporter Alicia Chang. "I just want to let people know that there's a way to survive West Nile."

Raney, who does not consider himself politically active, stepped far outside his comfort zone when he went to Sacramento in March 2005 to ask for $300 million in West Nile funding. He has also appeared in public service announcements with health officials from a mosquito control agency, been profiled in a documentary on the consequences of the disease, and provides counseling to West Nile victims and their families. "I'm willing to do whatever I have to do, go wherever I have to go, to get the message out," he told Chang.

Paul Rusesabagina/Hotel Rwanda

In 1994, in the African nation of Rwanda, nearly one million people were killed in the space of just 100 days. Thanks to Paul Rusesabagina's courage and compassion, 1,268 human lives were spared when the innkeeper sheltered them from the massacre in the Hotel Mille Collines, where he was manager.

The tensions began back in 1916, when Belgian colonists deemed the Tutsi ethnic group superior to the Hutus and granted the Tutsis better jobs and more advantages. The tables turned when Rwanda became independent in 1962 and the Hutus took power, which in turn led to a Tutsi rebel movement. On April 6, 1994, the plane carrying Hutu president Juvenal Habyarimana was shot down. The Hutus retaliated by slaughtering every Tutsi they could find.

Paul, who is of both Hutu and Tutsi descent, and his wife Tatiana, a Tutsi, fled for their lives to the hotel. Initially, his concern was to protect his immediate family. But when desperate

Tutsis appeared at his door, he couldn't bring himself to turn them away. So the hotelier left his comfort zone of personal safety. With no water or electricity, he kept 1,268 men, women, and children alive – in a hotel designed to accommodate 200 people – for 78 days. And when he was given the opportunity to leave on a UN truck with his family, he declined. As he told Oprah Winfrey in the March 2006 issue of her magazine, "The day before, some of my people had come to me and said, 'Listen, Paul, we've heard you're leaving us. If it's true, tell us so we can go to the roof and jump. We don't want to be killed with machetes.' Later that day, I made a decision. I had to tell my wife and children that I would send them to a safe place – but without me."

This Bigger Game was thrust upon Paul Rusesabagina against his will, and he rose to the challenge to become a hero celebrated in the 2004 film, *Hotel Rwanda*. As he said to Oprah, "If I left, the people in the hotel would be killed – and I would never be able to eat and feel satisfied or go to bed and rest again... If we want to play – if we want to change the world – we must first show up on the field to score."

Cindy Sheehan/anti-war activist
In April 2004, Cindy Sheehan's son Casey was killed in Iraq. A little more than a year later, the grieving mother set up camp outside George W. Bush's Crawford, Texas, ranch for the month of August in a quest aimed at bringing the President to terms with the consequences of America's involvement in Iraq.

"I want him [Bush] to tell me just what was the noble cause Casey died for?" she declared. "Was it freedom and democracy? Bullshit! He died for oil. He died to make your friends richer. He died to expand American imperialism in the Middle East."

Sheehan had no clue that her action would spark the enormous movement that it did. Her bold action proved to be a lightning rod for the questions and sentiments of millions of Americans. Spontaneous support arose around the country, discussions of her stand tore through the Internet and the press, and thousands of people jumped in their cars and drove to Crawford to join the encampment. Protest songs and shouts of solidarity from Sheehan's army of allies filled the nights there. And Camp Crawford sparked thousands of phone calls, e-mails, and statements of support. As the news spread, people all over the country debated this story and consequently, issues around the war in Iraq, thanks to Sheehan's bold stand for peace.

Born of grief, anger, and "No, not that," Camp Crawford was a movement that touched America. And it transformed Cindy Sheehan into a powerful spokesperson for peace on earth.

Eve Ensler/body image

Ever since playwright Eve Ensler brought her one-woman show, *The Vagina Monologues*, to the stage in the mid-1990s, she has struck a chord with women around the world seeking freedom from negative views of sexuality and body image issues.

The feminist activist was inspired to play a Bigger Game and write the play after being shocked by how a friend described her body in a discussion of menopause. Drawing on more than 200 interviews, Ensler chronicled how women felt about their intimate anatomy and turned these narratives into "poetry for the theater."

Ensler traces her efforts to help women love their bodies and end violence against women back to her own physical and sexual abuse at the hand of her father. "I don't know if I had not been a person who had survived enormous abuse if I'd be committed the way I am committed to this," Ensler told CNN.

Ensler's most recent play, *The Good Body*, is the result of interviews with women from different countries on how they transform their bodies to fit into their cultures. Ensler is also working on a version of the *Monologues* based on discussions with teenage girls so that the body image issue is addressed at a pivotal time in the development of young women's bodies.

The playwright and author said she longs for the day when she will no longer need to tell her stories. "I hope there's a time when *The Vagina Monologues* goes out of business. [That] there'll be a day when women literally can put on the shortest skirt and tightest top and feel good and that everyone will look at them with great appreciation and enjoyment and no one will hassle them or make them feel bad or insecure or threatened."

Bono and Bill and Melinda Gates/the Biggest Game of all – ending world poverty in our lifetime

In December 2005, the rock star Bono and billionaires Bill and Melinda Gates were named *Time Magazine*'s Persons of the Year. Why?

This alliance, said *Time*, is "unlikely, unsentimental, hard nosed, clear-eyed, and dead set on driving poverty into history. The rocker's job is to be raucous, grab our attention. The engineers' job is to make things work. 2005 is the year they turned the corner, when Bono charmed and bullied and morally blackmailed the leaders of the world's richest countries into forgiving $40 billion in debt owed by the poorest; now these countries can spend the money on health and schools rather than interest payments – and have no more excuses for not doing so. The Gateses, having built the world's biggest charity, with a $29 billion endowment, spent the year giving more money away faster than anyone ever has, including nearly half a billion dollars for the Grand Challenges, in which they asked the very best brains in the world how they would solve a huge problem.... For being shrewd about doing good, for rewiring politics and re-engineering justice, for making mercy smarter and hope strategic and then daring the rest of us to follow, Bill and Melinda Gates and Bono are *Time*'s Persons of the Year."

The Gateses' commitment acts as a catalyst, said *Time*. They need drug companies, major health agencies, churches, universities, and politicians to line up behind the world anti-poverty effort. Although the Gateses' pockets are very deep indeed, they need other organizations and countries to step up if poverty is to be abolished in this generation. Bono aids hugely in the campaign through his skill in bringing all the players to the field. There is no power broker on earth that he won't talk to, leveraging the influence and visibility that come with being the most famous rock star in the world. He charms, cajoles, and cites hard facts – whatever it takes to get the major players into the game. The rock star and the Gateses share a common compelling purpose: every life has equal value, and their hunger to change the world is, indeed, changing the world.

Bigger Game examples of *Something is missing*
Sometimes we look into the field and it becomes clear that something is missing. Neighbors don't have a place to congregate with one other. Cancer research results are not consolidated or widely available. There is plenty of food and plenty of hungry people and the former isn't reaching the latter. Teachers are not getting the recognition and remuneration they need to stay motivated and to attract the very best to the profession. Our hunger to provide what's missing becomes the wake-up call to action.

President John F. Kennedy/man on the moon
In 1960, President John F. Kennedy announced to the world that the United States of America would send a man to the moon by the end of the decade. At that time, the technology did not exist to make this Bigger Game happen. Scientists and engineers did not know how to achieve this stunning goal. Kennedy's challenge represented the intersection of his personal hunger to lead America to undisputed global leadership in science and technology with the hunger of his country (the field) to be first and best at pretty much everything. The compelling purpose that emerged from this intersection might be summarized in astronaut Neil Armstrong's words as he descended onto the lunar surface in June 1969: "One small step for [a] man; one giant step for mankind." And the whole world watched in wonder.

Clearly, comfort zones had to be abandoned in the search for breakthrough technology. Gulp after gulp after gulp had to happen as NASA contemplated how to get human beings to the moon and back safely with the world scrutinizing every step. The project required massive investments of time, money, resources, and faith. Bold action showed up from the moment President Kennedy declared his country's intention until the astronauts of Apollo 11 splashed down into the Pacific Ocean. The project couldn't have happened without thousands of allies, including the American taxpayer. (By the way, the USSR, America's competitor in the space race, was a huge ally in spurring us on.)

The program was designed in such a way that the space

program has been sustained – over numerous iterations – to this day. And assessment had to happen at every stage of the project; the constant return to "Where are we?" and "What's next?" is what made the June 1969 launch possible. Finally, the man-on-the-moon project transformed the United States of America into the undisputed technology leader of the Western world. And major discoveries, skills, and leadership roles were born and grown in direct response to Jack Kennedy's bold challenge to the American people.

Bob Nixon/Anacostia river project

The Anacostia River that runs through Washington, D.C., has been as blighted and trash-strewn as the neighborhood on its banks. Thirteen years ago, Bob Nixon took over a nonprofit organization dedicated to cleaning up the river – and soon realized that the youth living in the violent slum adjoining the polluted water were in just as much danger as the river itself. So Nixon's compelling purpose became a double clean-up mission. He enlisted neighborhood kids to help restore the river, giving them a sense of purpose and a love of nature in the bargain. Nesting eagles and osprey have returned to the riverbanks, and Nixon has seen many of his volunteer crew go on to college. His next goal is to raise $25 million to open an environmental education academy for at-risk kids. "Helping 40 of them at a time isn't good enough," the former film producer told *People* magazine. "In Anacostia alone there are 2,200 unemployed men and women between the ages of 17 and 25, and hundreds of them are on our waiting list."

Sasha Bowers/day-camp for homeless children

Fifteen-year-old Sasha Bowers, who lived in homeless shelters in Columbus for much of her childhood, is now a driving force behind a summer day-camp program in her hometown. She hungers passionately about making sure other kids can enjoy such activities as fishing and gardening. Bowers' future plans include attending law school and continuing to advocate for children.

Jimmy Carter/The Carter Center

Some retirees focus on improving their golf game. Not so retired US President Jimmy Carter, whose impact for his efforts to build peace, sufficiency, and democracy on Planet Earth is unprecedented among US presidents emeritus.

Jesus taught that the foundation of greatness is service to others. In December 2002, when Carter accepted the Nobel Peace Prize, it was clear that America's 39th president, a devout Christian, practices what Jesus preached.

Equipped with spiritual strength, organizational skills, and international experience, Carter has tackled intractable problems in the world's most volatile places, leading efforts to eradicate diseases such as guinea worm and river blinder, directing programs to boost harvests in depleted countries, and launching an urban rehabilitation program in Atlanta, among other initiatives of the Carter Center, which he founded with his wife, Rosalynn. The Carter Center has an ambitious mission – to advance human rights and alleviate human suffering for the people of the world – and it is making extraordinary headway thanks to the Carters' ambitious Bigger Game.

A pioneer in monitoring elections to ensure due process, Carter has helped facilitate the transition to democracy in such places as Panama, Haiti, and Nicaragua. He has helped mediate disputes, civil wars, and political transitions in countries including Ethiopia, North Korea, and Bosnia.

To admirers, Carter is America's global conscience. He is also a powerful example of what's possible when you set your mind and heart to it. "We'll never know whether something new and wonderful is possible unless we try," Carter told *AARP Magazine*. This is one politician who heard the call of "this must be and it must be me" – and took it to heart.

Adrian Bradbury and Kieran Hayward/Toronto Guluwalk

Their orange jerseys were eye-catching. Hundreds of women and men with T-shirts reading "Guluwalk" strolled through the streets of Toronto to publicize the plight of children in northern rural Uganda who avoided abduction by the rebel army by commuting

10-12 kilometers on foot to large cities. Adrian Bradbury and Kieran Hayward launched Guluwalk, a charitable organization that uses the power of sport to educate and engage Canadians in Africans' battle against poverty, famine, and disease. Bradbury founded the organization and Hayward serves on its board. United in their compelling purpose to improve the lives of Africans, Bradbury and Hayward, along with their cause, are known all over Canada.

William Hibbard/free wheelchair mission
"You may say I'm a dreamer, but I'm not the only one. I hope someday you will join us, and the world will live as one." – John Lennon

Imagine: the 100 million disabled people in developing countries, who today must crawl on the ground, suddenly riding around in wheelchairs. That's the goal of Free Wheelchair Mission, endowed by the efforts of William Hibbard, a long-time marathon runner, who undertook a cross-country trek to raise money to deliver 25,000 wheelchairs worldwide. Titled "Imagine: a Run Across America," Hibbard ran 52.5 miles a day, the equivalent of two marathons, to raise awareness of the urgency of the developing world's disabled population. Hibbard named the campaign after John Lennon's song, "Imagine." "I realized how Lennon's song took a simple idea and inspired millions of people. The one thing God gave me is a pair of sturdy legs that can run well, and if I can run and help get people wheelchairs, then I've done my small part," he said.

Rich and Yvonne Dutra-St. John/Challenge Day
Spurred by their own challenging, often humiliating high school experiences, husband and wife Rich and Yvonne Dutra-St. John founded the Challenge Day program in 1987 because they yearned to demonstrate how a school community could be given a little compassion and respect.

Their daylong program creates a safe, nurturing environment where students can embrace their commonalities as well as their differences – and really get to see into one another's hearts. The workshop uses games, small group discussions, and other activities to address issues that include bullying, violence, drugs, stereotypes, abuse, and racism. Teachers and staff participate along with the students. Trained Challenge Day leaders partner with school staff and students to lead the programs and conduct follow-up activities to give the experience real staying power.

To date, more than 2,300 Challenge Day programs have been presented across the U.S. and Canada, affecting the lives of more than 235,000 teenagers. The program has received international recognition. Following the senseless shooting in Columbine High School in Colorado, Rich and Yvonne were invited to bring the Challenge Day program to help the healing process. In 2000, Paramount Pictures made a 90-minute documentary, *Surviving High School*, which featured the program. And in November 2006, Oprah Winfrey exposed the Challenge Day program to millions of viewers on her popular daytime talk show.

"We are proud of how many people we have touched over the years, and yet one of our biggest dreams has been to get our message out to the masses. It is imperative to us that people around the world know that every child can and must live in a world where they feel safe, loved, and celebrated," said the Dutra-St. Johns of the compelling purpose that has stirred them to bold move after bold move.

Robert Redford/Sundance/environmental impact
Robert Redford has played two major Bigger Games in the last three decades, both connected to the land in Utah's mountains that he loves. When Redford bought two acres in Utah in the early 1960s, he was simply an actor who loved to ski. Since then, he has become a movie star, a producer, and an Oscar-winning director. But his signal achievements have always been linked to the land in Utah that now totals 6,000 acres. It inspired his staunch environmental advocacy and became the headquarters for Sundance, his incubator for independent filmmakers.

On the environmental front, Redford has lobbied effectively for the Clean Air Act, the Energy Conservation and Protection Act, and bills that regulate strip mining. His efforts to serve and support independent filmmakers and their industry have been equally stellar. Sundance is among the very few organizations that can credibly claim to have pioneered a market: the market for independent film, which continues to thrive against the competition of major Hollywood blockbusters and budgets. As critic Roger Ebert once said about Redford, "No one in recent movie history has had a more positive influence on new directions in American films."

Sundance is not a work of art so much as it is an organization with employees, budgets, and multiple commercial and noncommercial arms – and it mirrors Redford's entrepreneurial mind. "When you have the good fortune to have success in your life," he told *Inc. Magazine* in September 2003, "…that is precisely the time you should reinvent yourself. You should go right back to zero as though nothing had happened and start over. Because you can get real stale. You can fall in love with yourself or get to that danger point when you could ride on that success or try to repeat it. Repetition makes me nervous… there's no end game at Sundance… it's still evolving and it's meant to keep evolving."

Bigger Game examples of *Yes, more of that!*
Sometimes we glimpse something wonderful and crave more of that. A vision for cooperative community development based on principles of sustainability. One summer evening concert in the park that could blossom into a nightly event. A public transportation system that really works. Our hunger to create more of what's already working becomes our wake-up call to action. The following Bigger Game players hungered for *Yes, more of that!*

Ward Powers/Power of One
Early one morning in April 2002, a middle-aged attorney and father of three from Michigan awoke from a sound sleep with an urgent compulsion: to make a movie. Ward Powers immediately called his cousin Diane and best friend Scott to lend a hand. None of them had the slightest experience in filmmaking.

All they knew initially was that their film would involve asking questions to people from all walks of life to get many perspectives on a single theme: We Are All One. The amateur filmmakers felt deeply that even if they had no experience, equipment, or budget, their compelling purpose – raising awareness around the power of one – would carry them through.

And it did. Over the next two years, incredibly, the trio managed to interview many of the great spiritual thinkers of the world. Renowned authors, religious leaders, celebrities, scholars, and icons unexpectedly opened their doors to the "Circle of Bliss team," sharing their wisdom in the cause of "One."

The result was a combination of story and documentary that promotes themes of spiritual awareness and integral thought while advancing the evolution of human consciousness. And three amateur filmmakers from Michigan are amateurs no more.

Robin Ferst Howser/childhood literacy
Robin Ferst Howser was a successful commercial mortgage lender in Morgan County, Georgia. Then she read about Dolly Parton's literacy program, which donates books to Tennessee children, and quit her job on the spot to launch the Ferst

Foundation for Childhood Literacy.

Reading had been dear to Robin's heart from an early age, where she compensated for a hearing loss by devouring book after book. Knowing firsthand the difference that books can make for very young children, Robin set herself an audacious goal: to give every child in Georgia a book for every month of life from birth until age five.

At first, even finding the newborns was challenging. Undeterred, Robin began spending a good chunk of her weekends outside grocery stores and discount centers to register families for her program. Thanks to her perseverance, Robin's literacy initiative now includes a newsletter, parents' guide, and library card. Since its inception in 2000, the program has reached 25 out of 159 counties in Georgia, with 10,000 books mailed monthly. In Robin's own county, kindergarten readiness test results jumped from a 45 percent pass rate in 2001 to 80 percent in 2003. And Robin has become the author of a new generation enjoying the rich tradition of the bedtime story.

Christine Podas-Larson/Public Art Saint Paul

Never in her wildest dreams did Christine Podas-Larson ever imagine that one day she would be a rock star. But that moniker describes her pretty well these days. As founder of Public Art Saint Paul in Minnesota's capital city, Podas-Larson was a driving force behind "Minnesota rocks! The International Stone Carving Symposium" held in the summer of 2006. The project was but one in a long string of successes for an organization committed to change the face of a city by involving artists in every aspect of public works. Since 1987, Podas-Larson has partnered with artists, public agencies, private organizations, and community groups to commission works of art for public places. Her organization also works with artists to shape public places and structures, including parks, plazas, streetscapes, bridges, and gardens.

Podas-Larson's compelling purpose – to have artists' hands in city works – was fired back in college. Working in community affairs at a Saint Paul bank, she led the effort to bring original works of art by local artists into the bank. Subsequently, she formed Art Acquisitions, Inc., to develop art collections for major corporations. It was in this role that she worked with the St. Paul companies to curate a major art exhibit that focused on the Mississippi River. "The exhibit had a direct impact on the city and its view of itself, leading to a study of public art programs all across the country," said Podas-Larson. "The study recommended that for art to happen in the public sphere, a separate, independent, nonprofit organization needed to be formed. Public Art Saint Paul is that organization."

Ryan Hreljac/a well in Uganda

You are never too young to play a Bigger Game! One day, six-year-old Ryan Hreljac came home from his first-grade class in Toronto all charged up. He had learned that people in Uganda, Africa, don't have clean water to drink, and he wanted $70 so that a well could be dug. His parents offered him the chance to earn the money with extra chores, and Ryan went to work.

When the little boy surpassed his goal, he and his mother took his cash-full cookie tin to a local relief organization called Water-Can, only to learn that an actual well would cost considerably more – around $2,000. Unfazed, Ryan went back to work. His chore money accumulated slowly. But then, a few local newspapers ran stories about his project and a TV station followed suit. Soon Ryan had $1,000 in the cookie tin, but he was still just halfway to his goal. And then the Canadian Development agency matched his contribution and the $2,000 was in hand.

Ryan was invited to a special WaterCan meeting where he met Gizaw Shibru of Uganda. Ryan told Shibru he wanted his well drilled near a school. Shibru explained that the well would be dug by hand, because even a small drill cost $25,000. So, Ryan went back to his now familiar routine of fund-raising for the cause he believed in so deeply. After his homework each day, Ryan made presentations to service clubs and did television interviews. The donations poured in.

In 1999, Ryan received word that his well was helping many thirsty people. He was thrilled. He wanted to see it. On New Year's Day, some neighbors arrived with an envelope containing all their airline frequent flyer miles. The next summer, as Ryan and his parents approached a Ugandan village in the back of a pick-up truck, they heard chanting. They listened closely. Hundreds of people along the roadside were chanting Ryan's name. When the party arrived at the school, they were greeted by children and village elders, who escorted Ryan to the well. It was adorned with flowers and inscribed "Ryan's well, Funded by Ryan H." Ryan drank deeply.

In his short lifetime, Ryan Hreljac's hunger to alleviate suffering in a country far from his own has grown him in ways his parents could never have imagined. He has become an accomplished fund-raiser and public speaker, and an empowered advocate for transformation. When you add in the grand adventures he has had along the way, the evidence is clear. Playing a Bigger Game is about the biggest fun a person can have, at any age.

Angelina Jolie, Brad Pitt, and Dr. Jeffrey Sachs/Leveraging influence to create Millennium Villages

Angelina Jolie and Brad Pitt may be charismatic movie stars, but stardom is not their Bigger Game. Rather, they are setting a trend among celebrities by using their fame and clout to aid relief efforts in countries they care about around the world. For example, their New Year's Eve resolution for 2007 was to step up efforts to ease the economic and health crises of Cambodia, the homeland of their five-year-old son, Maddox. Their program, the Maddox Jolie-Pitt Project, has donated millions of dollars to the campaign and is partnering with Dr. Jeffrey Sachs and his antipoverty organization, Millennium Promise, to create the first Millennium Village in Cambodia.

Working together, Jolie, Pitt, and Sachs are creating an economic development program in northwestern Cambodia. Some 70 workers from the Maddox Jolie-Pitt Project are collaborating with Sachs's group to plant rice, distribute bed nets to fight malaria, create school meal programs, and provide medicines for clinics. The result will be a Millennium Village, wherein Sachs works with local governments to evaluate the specific needs of a region and help residents become self-sufficient within five years. There are already 78 Millennium Villages in Africa, and this collaboration will mark the first such project in Cambodia.

Kathleen Hummel, Our Little Haven

St. Louis social worker Kathleen Hummel was constantly frustrated in her work with older children in foster care, whose many disadvantages were only compounded by the challenges of adolescence. Knowing that nurturance, support, and guidance needed to kick in far earlier in these children's lives, Kathleen began searching for resources – and came up lacking. So she and her husband, Scott, took matters into their own hands. Starting from scratch, they did extensive research and networking in the field before applying for not-for-profit status. Finally, in 1993, the pregnant Kathleen and her husband, still in their 20s, both quit their jobs to open Our Little Haven.

The facility nurtures very young children until a juvenile court can reunite them with family or place them in permanent homes. The average stay in this homey space is about eight months – and the average transformation is extraordinary. "It's a healing environment," Kathleen told *Traditional Home* magazine. "Most children blossom and are ready to move on to a family setting."

Kathleen and Scott were driven by their hunger for these children to have a brighter future. And they were guided by a faith that only grew as the universe provided everything they needed to make Our Little Haven flourish. "We had youth and naiveté on our side," Kathleen told *Traditional Home*, "but we also had a much bigger hand behind us, supporting us."

Ivan Suvanjieff and Dawn Engle/PeaceJam

In the summer of 1994, artist and musician Ivan Suvanjieff was chatting with gang members on the streets of his gritty North Denver neighborhood when he discovered that they knew all about Archbishop Desmond Tutu and Nelson Mandela. It hit Suvanjieff that if these kids could actually meet somebody like Tutu, could they be inspired enough to get off the streets and help to improve their community?

The artist pondered this question for months with little hope that people of Desmond Tutu's caliber would make the trip to talk to these Colorado street toughs. And then he met Dawn Engle, the youngest woman ever to serve as chief of staff of a U.S. senator, who had gotten to know the Dalai Lama in the course of her work with the Free Tibet campaign. The two of them scraped together their last dollars to travel to India for an audience with His Holiness. It was worth it, because the Dalai Lama promised to participate if the pair could get ten other Nobel Peace Prize laureates to get involved, too.

So the two borrowed funds and began cold-calling Nobel Peace Prize winners around the world – and succeeded in signing on 11 of them for the project. But what, indeed, was this project? Suvanjieff envisioned youth coming together to share thoughts, experiences, and ideas for improving their local communities. It reminded him of musicians convening for a jam session, except this would be young people coming together to jam around peace. He called the program PeaceJam, and he and Engle identified a compelling purpose: to inspire a new generation of peacemakers who would transform their local communities, themselves, and the world.

PeaceJam is a program in which students participate in ongoing leadership training, study the lives and work of the Nobel Peace Laureates, attend two-day PeaceJam conferences led by the Nobel Laureates, learn wisdom and strategies for dealing with conflict, and implement service projects in their own communities.

The intention was that each PeaceJam participant would have a ripple effect, and that has proved to be the case. Since its inception, PeaceJam has grown into an international education program built around the participation of Nobel Peace Prize winners, who work personally with young people to teach peacemaking skills, pass on wisdom, and arouse hope. Since the program began, more than 200,000 young people have participated in more than 100 conferences and other events through the program, which has spread throughout the world. An unprecedented 14 Nobel Peace Prize Laureates serve on PeaceJam's board of directors and participate actively in the program. And evaluations reveal that 97% of participants believe that because of their experience with the program, they will be peacemakers for the rest of their lives.

Ivan Suvanjieff and Dawn Engle founded PeaceJam together, but their Bigger Game didn't stop there. In 2001, Archbishop Desmond Tutu himself married the two activists in South Africa.

Bigger Game Examples in Organizations
Corporations play Bigger Games – games that go far beyond simply making a profit for shareholders. For example, Southwest Airlines is committed to democratize the skies by becoming the low cost alternative for air-travelers and the world's best company to work for. Google is not only reorganizing the way the world gains access to information (no small game, that), but is also committed to providing its computer scientists with challenges so complex and fascinating that they will keep them deeply engaged for a decade or more. Twenty years ago, supercomputer giant Cray Research set out to make the biggest, fastest scientific computers in the world – and succeeded. Wal-Mart has undertaken a massive organics and sustainability initiative for employees and customers alike. These companies are successful businesses, and they are responding to a hunger in "the field" to make differences that extend well beyond their basic business domains. The bottom line that they adhere to is a triple one: passion, purpose, and profit. Following are some examples of Bigger Games being playing in organizations.

High-tech company/living the values
A sales executive with a large high-tech company brought her leadership team together for a Bigger Game workshop in order to create a clear objective that the whole team could connect to and own. After two and a half intense days of work, the team chose "Living Our Values" as the name of their Bigger Game. These values are:

* Be dedicated to our clients' success.
* Create innovation that matters to the company and the world.
* Honor all relationships with trust and personal responsibility.

The team devised three strategies for playing their game:

1) To make sure "everyone knows our game" by spreading the word to colleagues and clients.

2) Create community so that all the people on the team really get to know each other personally.
3) Create a "values at work" mentality, wherein managers change the language of their measurements and awards to underscore the importance of the values.

Plying these strategies, the team worked to be inclusive and creative. Those who attended the workshop aligned with those who hadn't. Many sellers reframed existing client relationships and created new ones based on the values. Awards were given based on how the sales team demonstrated dedication to clients, innovation that matters, and trusting relationships.

Today the team is using the Bigger Game to continue challenging themselves to recognize and leave comfort zones. As the team moves forward, it is paying careful attention to sustainability of the game.

A year after launching their game, the team surpassed all their colleagues in revenue, signings, and profits. Their client satisfaction ratings were the highest in their industry group and the organizational climate was rated the best as well. People love working in and with this team, and other divisions are noticing the successes and want some of that same energy and focus for their own teams. Now that they have faith in what is possible, the leaders of this team are eager to embrace bigger challenges in service of their Bigger Game as it morphs.

Mats Lederhausen/McDonald's

By age 35, Mats Lederhausen was running McDonald's Sweden, where he was paying close attention to preserving the environment, promoting nonviolence, integrating different ethnic groups, and employing people with mental and physical disabilities.

Still, he told *What Is Enlightenment?* magazine (March-May 2005), "...I realized that if tomorrow were the last day of my life, I wouldn't want to live it the way I was living. I began to ask myself 'What am I supposed to do?'"

So Ledenhausen approached McDonald's top management in the US with his vision of what business could be and the notion of duplicating what he was already doing in Sweden on a global basis. To his astonishment, they hired him as global vice president for strategy. In the last five years, the corporation's "social responsibility efforts are amplified and enhanced," Lederhausen said. "The goals, objectives, and actions we are taking are both more effective and more transparent than before – from trans-fatty acid reduction, eventual elimination of hormones and antibiotics in beef to waste reduction and water purification issues around the world...."

Lederhausen has now moved on to run the collection of brands known as McDonald's Ventures, where he is focused on "triple-bottom-line approaches – profit, community, and environment."

"My ultimate dream," he told *Enlightenment*, "is to manage a set of businesses that are all born out of a purpose bigger than their product... I am tired of going to meetings where spiritual people talk about how the world can be a better place but with very little evidence of any tangible outcome... Maybe I'm impatient... but I like to see physical manifestations of spiritual intent. My greatest sense of spirituality or connectedness is when I'm with people who come together for a cause much larger than themselves and do great things."

John Mackey/Whole Foods
"Wake up! Open your heart wider. Extend care and compassion further." So Whole Foods founder John Mackey told *60 Minutes* in a 2006 profile of the groundbreaking chain of health-oriented supermarkets.

Mackey's Bigger Game has been to create a new approach to growing a business dedicated to quality treatment of employees, customers, and the animals that die to nourish human beings. He has created an open, democratic structure for the company in which the workers vote on who to hire, share in profits, and know what everyone is being paid. His customers are drawn by the quality of Whole Foods' offerings and by the company's commitment to make food-shopping fun, engaging, and interactive. Appalled by the way animals are treated at factory farms, Mackey has also set new standards of care and compassion. "At the end of the day, quality of life is all we have. I do what I think is right," he told *60 Minutes*.

Mackey has always said no to "I can't." As a teenager, when he was cut from the basketball team at his Houston high school, his family moved to another neighborhood so Mackey could go to a different school where he was welcome on the team.

He opened his first health-food store after dropping out of college, and soon glimpsed an opportunity to expand the business thanks to a network of huge organic farms and regional distribution centers. Mackey has done more than his part in popularizing organic food in the US. Yes, it may be more expensive, but the food is "better-tasting, higher quality food that's better for health and for the environment," Mackey told *60 Minutes*.

Whole Foods donates 5% of its profits to charities. "The more profit we make," he said, "the more stores we can open and the more donations we can make. It's all interconnected."

In this Bigger Game, Mackey set out to create a kind of big business that America could trust. "I heard we were getting too corporate way back in 1982," he said. "But I haven't made any trade-offs."

Tex Gunning/Unilever Asia

"I don't want to live a life creating an illusion of meaningfulness while deep in my heart I know that every five seconds there is a child dying," says Tex Gunning, President of Unilever Bestfoods Asia. As reported in *What is Enlightenment?* magazine (March 2005), Gunning is putting Unilever's money where his heart is by placing the nutritional needs of children in the developing world at the core of Unilever's business mission.

Gunning built his career as a "restructuring expert" charged with firing people and selling off parts of the business. That's how he came to Unilever in 1995. There he decided he didn't want to spend the rest of his career firing people; instead, he found a compelling purpose in the commitment to make the workplace a "true human community" while growing a business. Indeed, reports *Enlightenment*, Gunning "created a unique culture where trust, honesty, and authenticity liberated a creativity that made the business soar. The results were one of the most dramatic business turn-arounds on record."

What follows are excerpts from *Enlightenment*'s interview with Gunning:

"Great leaders – and great companies – not only take care of stakeholders but also want to... leave the world better than they found it... it comes down to service. We as individuals should entirely integrate our personal lives and our search for meaning with our business lives. Businesses with a meaningful intent will bring meaning to the lives of their employees.

"I would love to make a difference in the lives of the unbelievably poor children in Asia. Their suffering is just unimaginable. I said to myself, I have no choice. We've got to do this. So we decided to start in India.

"The paradigm that divides the world into the social sector, the private sector, and the governmental sector... creates artificial barriers. We are each a constituent of the problem, so we have to combine our forces, our efforts, and our competencies... We all share this planet together; none of us can live a meaningful life when in Bangladesh, in China, in Darfur, hundreds of thousands of people are in need of help.

"If a few of us can prove that it makes good business sense not just to be socially responsible but to make a serious social mission intrinsic to one's business, then this is going to be written about, studied, and publicized. Because nothing is transferred faster than a success story in business. So I am very optimistic that if a few businesses can set an example here, we can make a tipping point out of it. And at this point, we really have no choice."

IBM and National Geographic/Mapping our Footsteps

Sometimes, Bigger Game players field a team of co-players before they even take the field!

In an unprecedented bold action, IBM and the National Geographic Society are partnering to map how humans populated Earth long before any written history. Arguably the most ambitious "genetic anthropology" research initiative in history, the Genographic Project will use advanced computer analysis of DNA from hundreds of thousands of people to reveal the deep migratory history of the human species. The project, said IBM CEO Samuel J. Palmisano, "promises to be a fascinating and possibly historic expedition into our collective past."

As part of the five-year partnership, field scientists will collect more than 100,000 DNA samples from 10 remote and isolated indigenous populations on six continents. These people's DNA is known to contain key genetic markers that have remained relatively unadulterated for hundreds of generations and thus provide reliable indicators of common lineage that can be used to trace human migration. With the samples in hand, IBM researchers will use sophisticated computer techniques to analyze that data and report the results. "We see this as the 'moon shot' of anthropology, using genetics to fill in the gaps in our knowledge of human history," said project initiator, leader, and National Geographic Explorer-in-Residence Dr. Spencer Wells.

People around the world can participate in the research effort by purchasing Genographic Project kits, submitting their own DNA samples, and allowing their results to be included in the database.

To spread the word on this historic effort, National Geographic and IBM are co-producing a one-hour television special each year on the National Geographic Channel.

Bernie Glassman/Greyston Bakery
The Greyston Bakery in New York is a $5 million business that makes elegant cakes sold at upscale restaurants, gourmet food shops, and on the Internet. But it doesn't hire people to make cakes. It makes cakes to hire people, people who are chronically unemployed.

Greyston, now run by Julius Walls, was founded in 1982 by Bernie Glassman, an aerospace engineer who became a Buddhist priest inclined toward social activism. "I wanted to show that people who are homeless, if given the chance and the right training, could not only work in our labor force but can produce the high niche items of our society," he said.

The entire bakery's profits – and Greyston is indeed profitable

– go into the Greyston Foundation, a nonprofit organization that runs programs for needy families in Yonkers, New York. The Foundation also receives grants and private donations, and offers programs that go well beyond bakery jobs, including computer classes, a clinic for people who are HIV positive, and low-rent housing.

The Greyston Bakery has expanded into a large new facility where more than 100 people are employed and profits are expanding.

"Do good and do well," said CEO Julius Walls of the thriving enterprise. "It's called a double bottom line. Our social mission is as important as our business mission."

Bigger Games of Bigger Game Workshop Participants

We have been delivering Bigger Game workshops around the globe since 2001. Many a Bigger Game has been started as a result of the workshop, and we highlight just a few of them here. Additional Bigger Games from workshop participants can be found by visiting www.biggergame.com.

Thomas/Habitat for Humanity

In May 2004, Thomas joined Habitat for Humanity-Brampton just in time to help with construction of their first home. He quickly became involved in building the home and moved into a leadership role on site, leaving his business for two months to assist in its completion. Shortly thereafter, he attended a Bigger Game workshop.

Then came the gulp. Thomas was appointed to chair the building committee. Through the Bigger Game workshop, he was encouraged to share his vision of building 10 homes for 10 families in 2006. The organization found the goal too ambitious and it morphed into seven houses by 2007. The gulp grew as Thomas led the successful charge to find building sites for the new homes; today, a three-unit townhouse is in the works.

Habitat for Humanity, a nonprofit housing program dedicated to eliminating poverty by building homes in partnership with families in need, has built more than 200,000 homes around the world to date. "With these numbers, why not 'homes for everyone by 2026?" said Thomas. Why not indeed?

"This birthing couldn't have occurred without the support of other Bigger Game players," Thomas said. "The continued inspiration and practice in living the model and hooking up with allies has kept my game alive and moving forward."

Conner/support groups for people with HIV/AIDS

Conner's Bigger Game is creating virtual support groups for people with HIV/AIDS in Nova Scotia, Canada. It is designed to help people break out of isolation – geographic, emotional, and social – and into a connected community of caring and support.

The project is supported by grants and includes tele-classes and in-person events, along with trained leaders and support materials. The model is community-based and self-sustaining.

Sandrine/Nourishing Our Children Campaign

Before she attended a Bigger Game workshop, Sandrine knew she was hungry for something – wanted a shift in her life – but she didn't have a structure for it.

A San Francisco-based learning specialist, she had become intrigued by a body of work on nutrition which suggested that many kids with learning disabilities are actually malnourished rather than disabled. She was teaching kids to read, but was hungry to get at the root of their problems. "This was a big 'no, not that' and I had a lot of passion," she said, "but I had no idea what to do with it."

Sandrine arrived at the Bigger Game workshop with a lot of passion, but she needed structure, a framework, and guidance. Once she located herself in the model and identified her compelling purpose – saving kids from eating the wrong types of foods – her passion immediately found a path.

Within 72 hours after the workshop ended, she received $75,000 from an individual donor, and by the end of the academic year, she closed her practice. As Sandrine started working within the model, she garnered allies and created a board of directors. She partnered with the Weston Price Foundation (which researches and advocates wise traditions in food, farming, and the healing arts) to partner as her fiscal agent. Everything unfolded in community, because "you just can't do it alone," she said.

In the campaign, Sandrine advocates that parents return to nourishing principles and traditional ways of preparing food, including eating at home around a table. The campaign began offering educational presentations to school and parent groups and a Web site. "Our goal is to make our message so compelling that people can't hear us and then go home to same old, same old. Enough people have changed now that we're over the top with joy," she said.

The first year of the campaign grew Sandrine's skills and tested her character. She had to learn how to create a PowerPoint presentation, lead a business meeting, work with numbers, run a board meeting, manage confrontation, and speak to large groups. "There were many moments when I thought this was too much of a stretch, that it was just too big," she said. "But when it got so hard I wanted to quit, my vision of kids being poisoned by the food they put in their bodies carried me through, time and again."

Julie/Young Entrepreneurs Alliance
"The Bigger Game workshop enabled me to work *on* my business rather than always be in it. It focused my intention on how I should be using my time, energy, and talent." So said Julie of Marlborough, Massachusetts, whose Bigger Game is the Young Entrepreneurs Alliance, an enterprise she started with her father to teach high-risk teens in vocational schools to operate their own businesses.

"Our compelling purpose is to help teens achieve economic independence," she said. "Our concept comes down to creating something I refer to as 'Me, Inc.' How do we show young kids that they have control of their lives and a portfolio of skills that are transferable?"

"It's really an ownership program," Julie continued. "These kids come from physical and psychological poverty. They haven't had jobs. We help them take the hypothetical stuff they're learning and turn it into a real business. And then they train the students in the class below them to be involved in the business, too. Participants in the program are focused and moving on to college and other training programs instead of dropping out."

Examples of the businesses the program has generated in Massachusetts high schools include graphic design, scanning, and virtual office assistant enterprises. Julie is looking to franchise the concept to make it widely available in other communities.

Julie says she came into the Bigger Game workshop backwards because she already knew her passion. "I wanted to use the model to create a framework for my passion in order to achieve sustainability," she said. "And, passion is contagious. I saw what my passion did for others and felt what theirs did for me."

Julie says she is taking greater risks from a more grounded

position since she began working from within the Bigger Game model. "The risk is not about me; it's about being able to discern what is important. Because it's about the game, not me, I don't take setbacks personally."

She also takes better care of herself thanks to the model. "You can't take a bold action if you're exhausted," she said. "You need to invest in yourself. It has taken me time to see that, because I'm a driven woman. But it has become completely obvious that I must practice sustainability in my own life. As a result, I'm better rested and my family is much closer. I tell you, staying in the Bigger Game model keeps my eyes on the prize in all kinds of ways."

Sue/Comedienne

Sue had a big corporate career, most recently with JP Morgan. Her life was "stuffed" and she hungered for something else, although she didn't know what. So she signed up for a Bigger Game workshop. Today, Sue is a comedienne. "It's humor with purpose – entertaining while it challenges people to make positive changes in life that will have them be more joyful and respond better to stress," she said.

While the compelling purpose of having people connect to their own creativity through the power of joy and humor has been a constant thread since the workshop, doing comedy was not Sue's first Bigger Game. "Leaving the workshop, I wondered how I could incorporate my compelling purpose into my current life, so I created a job description at JP Morgan that involved infusing the culture with more fun and innovation," she explained. "They were receptive to the concept, but one person wasn't enough to make the change."

Sue stayed hungry and curious. She heard about a comedienne named Loretta Laroche, who uses humor for everything from improving corporate teamwork to improving your outlook, and attended a performance. Sue knew she was interested in entertainment as a way to get her message out. So she reached out to connect with new allies through 20-some informational interviews. In the spring, she left JP Morgan with nothing lined up except her intense hunger. After taking a "vocational vacation," Sue started getting some material together and began to perform. "It was a big gulp every time I took the stage," she said. Then she began to partner with Loretta Laroche to create humor with purpose. "I had tried to live into my compelling purpose every way I could in a business setting," said Sue. "I finally knew it was about performing this material that helps illuminate the human condition."

Reflecting on the Bigger Game model, Sue said it helped her put one foot in front of the other and think things through. "The balance is tricky. It would have been great to veer off and go to film school, but I had to return to sustainability. But that can be too safe. I have to force myself to do something gulpy every week. And I have done lots of reaching out to allies and leaning into them. The model gives me a framework for channeling my action and best utilizing my resources. It's a directional way-finder. Without the Bigger Game, I could have spent another five years spinning my wheels at JP Morgan."

Instead, Sue has become more open, more expansive, and increasingly in the company of wildly creative people. "I am open to a whole new world of possibilities," she said.

Pat/Women's conference
When she left the Bigger Game workshop in 2004, Pat's Bigger Game was to hold the largest Women's Day Conference in San Mateo County in 2005. Mission accomplished. And topped the following two years. Pat's compelling purpose is to create a space where women from different social, economic, and ethnic backgrounds can come together and contribute to one another. Today, her Bigger Game has morphed as she works to create a venue for women leaders to support and enjoy one another.

Pat came to the Bigger Game workshop as a huge supporter of women's rights. Nothing was available in her county. She decided that "it has to be – and it must be me." Gulp. "It was scary to actually own it and ask others to join me. What if nobody showed up? And I had never raised money before – another gulp," she said.

Pat had to leave many comfort zones behind as she moved forward, particularly the comfort zone of working behind the scenes. Now she was on the front line, charged with inspiring others. And she had to invest in taking care of herself, because her game required lots of energy. "I am no longer fearful to ask for what I need," she says. "And I'm more confident, more willing to admit that I don't know, more humble, slower to judge, more open-minded, and way more curious."

Her game required myriad allies. She started by e-mailing everyone she knew, then networked like crazy to recruit the talents and skills she didn't have and to sign up sponsors. "Women from all segments of the community came to help. The Bigger Game is not about doing it alone; it has been a huge relief all over my life to know that there are other people yearning to come and play and contribute," she said.

During the conference, Pat found that the women got into deep conversation very quickly. The success of the venture led her to contemplate what else she and her allies could do in the community. Today, her Bigger Game is on the way to morphing into a nonprofit organization of world conversation cafes for women leaders.

Sustainability of her game has much to do with the many allies Pat brought into the fold. "In our committee, we work the model, consistently returning to hunger, compelling purpose, vision, and sustainability," she said. "This project has taken on an energy of its own."

Additional Bigger Game stories can be found by visiting
www.biggergame.com.

About the Authors

Laura Whitworth, co-founder of the Bigger Game, passed away on February 28, 2007, after a two-year courageous battle with lung cancer. In addition to the Bigger Game, she is also co-founder of The Coaches Training Institute, one of the first educational institutions to develop and offer coach training. At the time of this printing, more than 20,000 coaches have been trained by CTI.

Laura is also the co-author of the popular book *Co-Active Coaching: New Skills for Coaching People Toward Success in Work and Life*.

Rick Tamlyn is a sought-after leader in the human development field and works internationally as an experiential keynote speaker, workshop/seminar leader, and personal leadership coach. Using his own unique brand of wisdom, wit, and humor, Rick's experiential keynotes and workshops are interactive, dynamic, and entertaining. Rick has inspired and challenged thousands of people – both

individuals and Fortune 500 organizations – to achieve their personal and professional goals and make their dreams a reality.

Rick can be contacted by visiting www.RickTamlyn.com.

 **Caroline MacNeill Hall**, MA, is Partner in mac advisors, a leadership development advisory firm that provides executive coaching and assists functional teams to build positivity and productivity toward an energized, high-performance organizational climate. A practicing certified coach and a senior course leader for Coaches Training Institute (CTI), the world's premier coaching school, Caroline also leads CTI's flagship program, Co-Active Leadership, a highly experiential yearlong leadership incubator based in the U.S., Spain, and Japan.

In all her work, Caroline challenges individuals to discover their power and purpose and find meaningful vehicles for expressing both in the world.

To learn more about the Bigger Game and our workshop and trainings, please visit www.biggergame.com.

Play a Bigger Game

Comfort **Zones**	Hunger	*Compelling* Purpose
ASSESS	**BOLD** Action	GULP
SUSTAIN ABILITY	Allies	Investment

LaVergne, TN USA
26 January 2011
214029LV00003B/225/P